MISSING FROM ACTION

Weldon M. Hardenbrook

THOMAS NELSON PUBLISHERS
Nashville

Published in Nashville, Tennessee, by Thomas Nelson, Inc., and distributed in Canada by Lawson Falle, Ltd., Cambridge, Ontario.

Printed in the United States of America.

Scripture quotations are from THE NEW KING JAMES VERSION. Copyright © 1979, 1980, 1982, Thomas Nelson, Inc., Publishers.

Library of Congress Cataloging-in-publication Data

Hardenbrook, Weldon M.
  Missing from action.

  Bibliography: p. 186
  1. Men (Christian theology) 2. Men—United States.
I. Title.
BT702.H37   1987   261.8'3431   86-31166
ISBN 0-8407-3074-8

1 2 3 4 5 6 7 8—92 91 90 89 88 87

*I dedicate this book
to my father.*

CONTENTS

PREFACE ━━━━━━━━━━━━━━━━━━━━━━━━━━━

Over the years, I have had the privilege of working with the broad spectrum of men who can only be found in America. No matter who they have been—capitalists, Communists, college students, dropouts, Christians, atheists, blacks, whites, young, or old—they have had one problem in common: They have suffered, to one degree or another, from the touch of the feminizing forces that have taken over our land. These men have not been sure what it means to be a man.

Yet, the first time I ever lectured on the subject of why men are "missing from action"—after I had spoken for approximately an hour, followed by a time for questions—the men suddenly stood and applauded, not just polite applause but the kind that seemed to rejoice in finally hearing a viable answer to the aching question they had never vocalized.

Anyone who has consistently spoken before audiences knows those special moments when you have touched on a real need. That night gave special meaning to what I had already suspected—the American male is in a fundamental struggle for his identity.

Several years later, my wife and I spoke on this same subject to a group of men and women in Nashville, Tennessee. There, Mike Hyatt, a vice president of Thomas Nelson Publishers, enthusiastically echoed the same response as the other men who had heard these lectures. He agreed that I had hit on a raw nerve that was causing great pain. Mike and his wife prompted a commitment from me to put on paper what I had been saying to men for the past three years.

Now, although a significant reawakening has begun to take place among American men, there has been little yet produced that shows how a study of American history can provide answers for today's seeking men. It is to that end that I have written this book. How can a twentieth-century American male know what manhood really is? It is my hope that *Missing from Action* will assist in answering that question. As we look to the past, perhaps we can see the future!

Finally, people who write books all by themselves must have incredible talent. This project, to be sure, would not exist without the inspiration and sweat of some dedicated assistants.

I would first like to thank Terry Somerville, who sat by my side from beginning to end, writing, researching, and expanding on my assessment of the predicament of the American male.

In addition, I am grateful to my secretaries, Ivy Valory and Alice Hughes, who in the midst of many tasks were always willing to transform our barely legible notes into marvelous word-processor print-outs.

I am also indebted to Peter E. Gillquist, an extremely busy editor and church leader, who gave some crucial advice and whose input made for a more readable manuscript.

Oh, yes, one more thing. My thanks to Jerry Munk. It was his mention of the fact that the men of this land are feminized that became the catalyst for my research and, ultimately, led to this book you are about to read.

1

THE DEATH OF MASCULINITY

The great outpouring of words about the contemporary American woman these past few years has made it seem as though the male either had no problems or didn't count enough to have them aired.

Myron Brenton[1]

In 1963, feminist Betty Friedan informed us that "American women no longer know who they are."[2] In the years since then, there has been an absolute avalanche of literature, documentaries, talk shows, workshops, organizations, and political activism focused on the role and identity of women.

Now the male of the species is in turmoil.

Feminist rhetoric would have us believe that women have suffered far more than men. But statistics reveal a dramatically different story. In almost every way measurable, the stresses of modern life now seem more damaging to men than to women.

STATISTICS WE COULD DO WITHOUT

Look at substance abuse. The rates of alcohol and marijuana use are considerably higher in the male population than in the female population, according to government statistics. Six times more men than women are arrested for drug

9

abuse. For every woman arrested for drunkenness, more than ten men will be incarcerated. Over 88 percent of drunk drivers are men.[3]

In 1983, more than 83 percent of the people arrested for serious crimes were men. FBI crime statistics tell us we are over six and one-half times more likely to be murdered by a man than a woman. If your house was destroyed by arson, the chances are seven out of eight that the person who lit the match was a man. If your VCR was stolen, the odds are more than twelve to one that the thief was male.

Crime really is a male affair, as the population of American penal institutions shows. A man is twenty-five times more likely to end up in state or federal prison than a woman.

Not only do men live an average of seven years less than women, but they suffer far more than their female counterparts from ulcers and other stress-related diseases. Men are more likely than women to expire from cancer, pneumonia, liver disease, strokes, hardening of the arteries, and heart failure. In 1981, over 27,500 people in this country committed suicide. Almost 75 percent of these suicides were men.

Men are hurting. And yet pathetically little is being said or done to find the source of the problems that bedevil the twentieth-century American male.

THE UNKNOWN MAN

The vast ocean of attention devoted to women in recent years stands in stark contrast to the relative dribble of information available dealing with the crises facing men. What little information does exist tends to be viewed through a feminist prism.

Take, for example, the curricula offered to the 100,000 undergraduates of the University of California. At four of the university's nine campuses, one can earn a bachelor of arts degree with a major in women's studies. Yet none of the campuses offers a corresponding major in men's studies.[4] As of this writing, the university's intercampus library computer has 762 listings under the heading of "men" while under the heading of "women" there are 14,289 entries—1,800 percent more information about women than men!

One of the system's campuses, the University of California at Santa Cruz (USCS), is located near my home, and it offers women's studies. At the time of my research, virtually all of the program's twenty-seven professors, associate professors, and lecturers were women. Five of the ten required courses in the major could be chosen from certain broader related fields of studies. The required courses "must include a three-course sequence in feminist issues, method and theory."[5]

In the neighboring sociology department, there are undergraduate and postgraduate courses entitled "Sociology of Women," "Women in the Courts," "Women in Work," "Feminist Theory," and "Feminist Research Seminar." There is only one course on the sociology of men. Unlike its feminist counterpart, this course is offered only in alternate academic years.[6] The University of California curricula typify the way the subject of men is dealt with, or perhaps I should say ignored, by society in general.

POINTING THE FINGER

One thing you must understand before we go any further: This book has not been written to de-emphasize the American woman or to blame the ills of men on the rise of the feminist movement in the United States. The problems of men are their fault! They have lost their way to true manhood and thrown responsibility to the wind. Now they've reaped a whirlwind. If men refuse to be men, women will move into the roles of service and responsibility men have always filled in the past. Out of the need for survival and for the protection of their children, the mothers—not the fathers—of this nation

11

have been thrust into leadership roles in homes, schools, and churches.

This book will not attempt to define manhood in terms of chromosomes or *psyche* (this has already been done by many). Rather, when I speak of being a man, I am referring to being one who is responsible for moral leadership in home and society. This is not to say that women do not have a moral responsibility or are incapable of leadership. What I am saying is that the ultimate responsibility for moral leadership in human affairs has been the distinct domain of the male gender. It is my contention that the increasing failure of the American male to exercise this responsibility is the primary factor leading to the current confusion about what it means to be a man in twentieth century America.

A letter to Ann Landers illustrates the plight of families brought about by men "missing from action."

> Mother ran our family. Daddy was a wimp. If anyone is at fault, it's him. Almost all my teachers, from nursery to high school were women. The male teachers were all effeminate. In one school the only male employee was the janitor. I was disciplined and rewarded exclusively by women. I learned early where the power was and I wanted to be on the winning side.[7]

The man who wrote this letter is not atypical. Whether men like to acknowledge it or not, all of them have been feminized to one degree or another through similar circumstances. But when I write about being feminized, I am not talking about men who become homosexual or who, though heterosexual, have certain effeminate attributes. When I speak of feminization, I am referring to a conditioning process in modern American culture in which men have been trained to respond to people and situations in ways that are more akin to historical female behavior patterns than they are to historical male behavior patterns.

This feminizing process has evolved as the result of a series of dramatic events during the last two centuries, and a severe identity crisis has developed as a result. With an arrogant contempt for the consensus of history, there are those who have declared modern man "liberated" from "archaic" and "unfair" sex roles. But the pathetic smorgasbord of alternative identities now peddled everywhere from TV talk shows to church pulpits leaves men more confused than ever about what manhood means.

Let's face it. It's extremely difficult for men to act like men when so much confusion exists about the definition of manhood. For most of human history, people knew what it meant to be a man. Now, at least in modern America, no one seems to know. Modern cultural aberrations, if they have not dealt a death blow to the traditional understanding of masculinity, have certainly left it crippled. And yet, the crises that plague American men, women, and their families will not be solved without a return to historical masculinity.

Missing from Action will attempt to sound forth a call for such a return to manhood. In this book I will consider specific models of manhood, both the false and the true, and I will devote several chapters to a challenging and surprising study of manhood in early American history. I will pinpoint how and when the U.S. male lost his masculinity and note the factors that contributed to his being missing from action. Finally, I will propose a workable game plan to help America's men regain their identity.

2

FOUR FALSE ICONS

We evolve into the images we carry in our minds. We become what we see.

Jerry Mander[1]

Do you have any doubt about the power of images? Ask Walter Mondale. He's convinced he was beaten by one. Throughout the 1984 presidential campaign, Mondale was unable to overcome the image of President Reagan as a strong, capable leader, as the one who got America rolling again. Mondale argued that the real Ronald Reagan was not at all like his public image. But he argued in vain. The image presented by Reagan, however real or unreal, was far more appealing to the voters than the image Mondale presented. Reagan's historic landslide stands as a witness to the power of images in the minds of the people.

If you still aren't convinced about the power of image, ask the editor of *Seventeen* magazine, whose August 1985 edition contained 346 ads within its 400 pages! Or ask the president of McDonald's or Ford or Coca-Cola about the power of product images. As a former ad agency art director, I have witnessed firsthand how the continued success of the most stable companies hinges upon the image projected.

But the power of images affects more than our voting and

spending habits. Images affect our lifestyles as well. What we eat, how we dress, where we travel—and more important, what we believe and how we behave—are *all* heavily influenced by the images that surround us.

Images of American masculinity have been under intense scrutiny in recent decades. A cloud of uncertainty has settled in. What does it mean to be a man today? After whom does the American male pattern his life? Who are what I call the contemporary icons of masculinity? What are men supposed to look like, be like?

In lieu of the historical images of masculinity, modern American culture has fabricated at least four male stereotypes to fill the need for a model of manhood. Whether one considers them repulsive or attractive, there are at least four current choices before today's man.

1. MACHO MANIA: THE DUKE, DIRTY HARRY, AND RAMBO

In the history of motion pictures, few people have so firmly stamped their image upon the minds of American men—and women—as did the late Marion Michael Morrison. We knew him better as John Wayne, the film name he took so that he could project a more masculine image. And project it he did. With the added benefits of a large, muscular body and a deep, rough voice that carried the tone of someone who was in charge, Wayne was a perennial man's man. For more than four decades, the impact of his career intensely influenced the opinions of millions of men about what it meant to be manly. Though at age sixty-nine he had to don a toupee to do it, Wayne maintained his macho image through his very last film, *The Shootist*.

John Wayne always stood for principle over personal comfort. He became the hero and protector of the West, the flesh-and-blood embodiment of the American male who, without flinching, could always suppress his feelings of fear and pain in his relentless war against evil.

Face it. Most of us really liked Wayne. He overcame all obstacles and ensured survival in the American wilderness. Almost never a villain, with his hat tipped to God, he projected an aura of honesty and integrity that causes even present-day feminists to wish today's more youthful macho stars could be traded for the original macho man.

John Wayne's desire for the triumph of good over evil drove him to face life bravely and to be prepared to fight and die with honor, courage, and pride. For the Wayne model, stubborn pride was a virtue. Recall his line in the film *She Wore a Yellow Ribbon:* "Never apologize, mister, it's a sign of weakness."

Often portrayed as an independent man who could find life very satisfying without any ties to family or others, Wayne sat tall in the saddle *alone*. For all his positive qualities, his unbending arrogance set forth a tainted model of what it means to be strong, masculine. The Duke always maintained a cool countenance, staring straight ahead no matter how grim or tragic the calamities that surrounded him. Although a "good guy," he became a model for the big bad men to come.

And come they did, emphasizing some of the worst qualities of the Wayne stereotype!

Enter next Clint Eastwood—Mr. "Make my day" himself. He would rise above even Wayne's attempt to create the standard American macho image. As Eastwood himself confesses:

Everybody knows nobody ever stood in the street and let the heavy draw first. It's me or him. To me that's practical, and that's where I disagree with the Wayne concept. . . . I do all the stuff Wayne would never do. I play bigger-than-life characters, but I'll shoot a guy in the back. I go by the expediency of the moment.[2]

This six-foot-four man has squinted through thirty films in the last twenty years to become, as *Newsweek* magazine canonized him, "an American icon." Eastwood is even macho in his view of his trade: "Going with your gut is the Eastwood approach to acting," which, he says, "isn't an intellectual art at all. It's strictly animalistic. It comes out of an animal part of the brain."[3]

Like John Wayne, Clint Eastwood is afraid of no one. But unlike Wayne, Eastwood seems to have no respect for God. At least, that is the message the viewer receives. The old macho image was, "God, guts, and guns built America." But the new macho image is simply, "Guts and guns built America."

The new macho man can face any forbidding situation in life not only with the courage of Audie Murphy (America's most decorated soldier of World War II) but with the unfeeling soul of a robot. He doesn't cry, whine, complain, or worry. He only sweats! Not from fear, mind you, but from the exertion used to win against the unbelievable odds that challenge him.

The "macho mania" that lures millions of identity-impoverished American males to the box office today often invites them to see Eastwood's hottest challenger, Sylvester Stallone. His mission? Change our male images. Says he, "Screen characters seem more like young ladies than real men, and it's time to re-establish the balance."[4]

As the movie *Rambo* so vividly demonstrates, the new macho superhero is perfectly capable of single-handedly destroying half of North Vietnam, along with a contingent of Russian reserves, while at the same time intimidating his own government.

But there is a radical difference between the new macho man and the John Wayne prototype. The new macho challenges the traditional masculine image by removing its soul. The suffering state of the American male has driven the new macho man to create an image far beyond his potential to imitate. With frantic approval and exhilaration, the male moviegoer applauds the screen hero, only to return home with a sense of greater impotence.

17

The macho maniacs portrayed in film can't make it in the real world. Eastwood was right when he said that he played "bigger-than-life characters." Only the movie screen can contain them. But supermachos won't be the ones to balance the tilt of the masculine teeter-totter back to where it should belong. The stereotypes they are creating are as void of feeling as they are of fear.

2. THE GREAT PRETENDER: ARCHIE BUNKER

Archie Bunker. Need I say more? This character has incarnated an American stereotype that will be with us for a long, long time. Archie Bunker displayed his hilarious TV interpretation of the proud, urban, blue-collar, big-mouthed bigot before millions of viewers from 1971–79. Slouched in his easy chair, Archie captured a host of faithful fans. "All in the Family" was a series that touched the heart of almost every home and will last as long as the reruns continue to play. Perfectly on cue, this man could be polite and gracious to any woman except his own wife. In fact, it was important to Archie to "lovingly correct" his wife with a constant stream of contempt. He wanted all who observed them to have no doubt who was in charge. Here is just one example of his attitude toward her:

EDITH: Oh, Archie, I had the most wonderful idea!
ARCHIE: Never mind ideas. When did you ever have an idea? I don't need ideas, I need a beer.[5]

There he is. A man who gains a sense of personal worth by constantly belittling his family. That's Archie. His world is small, real small. But that doesn't prevent him from having a dogmatic opinion on everything and everybody.

I call Archie, the man, the "Great Pretender." He imagines he rules over his family and neighbors while everyone but

Edith ridicules him behind his back. He has convinced himself that courage and fearlessness are his seal. So popular is this characterization of the American male that CBS newsman Mike Wallace interviewed actor Carroll O'Connor to get some straight answers regarding the impact of "All in the Family."

WALLACE: What you're saying to me is that there are a lot of relationships in the United States that are very much like Archie and Edith?

O'CONNOR: That's what the mail tells us, yes. Occasionally some mail says the viewers don't believe something that Archie does or something Edith says. But by in large, it's "Boy, that's it! You've got it. The next-door neighbors; that's Uncle Harry; that's Aunt Flossie."[6]

It seems beyond understanding that any woman—on TV or in real life—would want to be married to a man who is constantly acting out the Archie Bunker fantasy. On the other hand, these great pretenders probably think they are lovable creatures. In reality they are frightened little boys who have crawled into their dreamworld as a protection against imagined enemies of their masculinity. Most are good hearts frantically trying to hold on to some tradition they don't quite understand.

Some men may intentionally try to be macho, but no one sets out to be an Archie Bunker. While few men would be willing to admit that Archie is a reflection of *their* masculinity we all know numerous *other* men that are flesh and blood incarnations of Archie. While we don't want him as a hero, he is a true image of large segments of American manhood. And it is precisely because the character is such a humorously accurate reflection of so many men that Archie has become so well known and an undeniable icon of one type of American masculinity.

Cartoon critics David White and Robert Abel are right when they say, "Archie Bunker, like it or not, is a role model, an example of an authority figure in the home. He and other foolish male characters too numerous to mention have distorted the image of husbands and fathers."[7]

Archie Bunker is simply another false, but funny, American male icon. He keeps his frightened domestic world at arm's length through a constant stream of caustic verbiage. Not knowing what true masculinity is, Archie, like many other men, pretends.

3. WORLD-CLASS WIMP:
DAGWOOD BUMSTEAD

Nobody likes to be called a wimp, but so many men fit the overly submissive male category that comic strip creator Chick Young decided to make daily entertainment of their plight. The strip he developed over fifty-five years ago, *Blondie,* is still the most popular and well read of the approximately 128 comics in the newspapers.

In *World Encyclopedia of Comics* author Maurice Horn says, "Blondie became a devoted wife and affectionate companion, as well as the actual head of the Bumstead household. While losing none of her charm she acquired solid virtues of pluck and level-headedness, and often has to rescue Dagwood from the many jams he gets himself into."[8]

Like the fathers in many other cartoons and television series, Dagwood is regularly the butt of jokes. So inept is he that a Temple University professor describes him as "a well-meaning idiot who is constantly outwitted by his children, his wife and even his dog."[9]

As with Archie Bunker, no one wants to be a Dagwood Bumstead. But also as with Archie, it is because Dagwood is such an accurate portrayal of so many men that he has been a mainstay of the comic section for over half a century. Dagwood may be a distasteful icon of American masculinity but he has been, and continues to be, an image of manhood nonetheless.

Oh, well, it's only the comics. Men need to be able to laugh at themselves, don't they? True. But have they given in to the characterization of the father as the hapless male that no one takes seriously? Is Dagwood a tragic figure rather than a comic one? I ask because the father more than any other male is singled out for special ridicule. "Strong men on television are either bachelors, widowers, or divorced, and the married men with children are portrayed as somewhat ridiculous, incompetent, and confused. Nobody could hate or fear the poor devils—a humane person could only pity them."[10]

If you think my cartoon example is a bit extreme, let me offer a personal example. My friend and I, as first graders, were great fans of Captain Marvel, a superhero of the forties. One of the comic books about him that we purchased with our hard-earned money made an offer we couldn't refuse. For one dollar we could send away for a cape and a magic ring like Captain Marvel's. The most exciting bonus to come with this special offer was the "secret word" that would enable us to do what Captain Marvel did. To us that meant we would have the ability to fly!

Each day we anticipated the arrival of our special package. Finally, it came. We quickly tore open our treasured delivery and draped its contents upon our backs. With capes on and the rings adjusted to our small fingers, we planted the secret word inside our minds.

Having already planned our strategy in advance, we swiftly climbed to the roof of a large two-story barn. Standing at the edge with arms held straight out in front of us, we surveyed our flight pattern and the location for touchdown. We rubbed our rings and said the magic word, "SHAZZAM!" We took a deep breath and leaped. It was childlike faith in the promise

21

of fantasy. Fortunately, about a foot of soft manure had accumulated in the old chicken pen below. Cut and badly bruised, we cried tears of pain and disillusionment as we ran home to two puzzled mothers. We had believed a lie.

The symbols created by clever men for comic strips do relate to our behavior. If not, why would a comic strip such as *Blondie,* which constantly portrays a bumbling man, be one of the favorites of the last half of this century? Why do men put up with this portrayal of the father as a bumbling wimp? Because men in America have given in to the wimp syndrome. Most of the millions of people who daily read this strip are men![11] Men have bought the image of themselves characterized by the comic strip and carried to even further lengths in current television situation comedies.

Not that the wimp is without virtue at all. Unlike the macho man or the pretender, he is usually a very sensitive guy. In fact, he's so tender he's been in line for every sensitivity seminar to hit town in the last fifteen years.

Don't worry about being offended by him. He's always *nice.* Somewhere he's found a modern beatitude: "Blessed are the passive, for they shall avoid conflict." And avoiding conflict is of paramount importance to the wimp. Under no circumstance would he turn over tables and drive out money-changers as Jesus did. He avoids a fight at all costs. Worse than Dagwood, he'll even let his family fall apart rather than confront forces that seek to destroy it.

David Frost, the British TV commentator, writes:

There's a curious double standard operating in America. In certain areas women have established an absolute stronghold . . . and men think that surrender is the only road to acclaim. But the letters I receive from women all around America are pleading for more male leadership. They feel that they've gotten too much dominance over their men, and that their men are mice, and they wish they'd get out and lead them a bit more. "I don't want my man to keep surrendering," these women say.

"But now," writes one woman observer, "male surrender has become a conditioned reflex in the USA."[12]

4. GENDER BLENDERS: MICHAEL JACKSON AND BOY GEORGE

According to *People* magazine, "A psychologist recently asked his 7-year-old nephew, 'Is Michael Jackson a boy or a girl?' The boy thought for a moment before replying, 'Both.'"[13]

The fourth false icon offered to American men is the most shocking and devastating assault on masculinity of all. It doesn't even pretend to be masculine. It is the image of androgyny, having female and male characteristics all wrapped into one but being really neither female nor male.

George Washington wore a wig, to be sure, but there was never any question about his masculinity. The same, however, cannot be said of the famous George of our day, bisexual rock star Boy George. Wholesale confusion of sexual identities has become typical of the eighties.

Gender blending used to be primarily the domain of rock music. Almost three decades ago Richard Penniman, known to the public as Little Richard, appeared on stage looking very unlike the typical teen-age male of the fifties. Steven Simels observes, "Throughout the Fifties, Richard was never seen or photographed without lipstick, the wildest hairstyles, and the heaviest eye makeup."[14]

Little Richard had many successors, some of whom were far more successful than he.

By the end of the sixties, the Rolling Stones

were exploiting the confusion between the macho and the effete for maximum shock value. Some of this was calculated, as in the famous 1966 group portrait of the band as World War II WAC nurses. . . . The high point of this particular phase is documented for eternity in the film *Performance*, where Mick Jagger portrays a retired rock star in the process of becoming a psychedelic ballerina.[15]

The rise of the homosexual rights movement and the assault on male roles by the feminist movement left the door open for the androgynous musicians of the seventies to occupy a position closer to music's mainstream. The most successful of these, David Bowie, is still a rock star today.

Although Bowie has recently retreated from overt gender blending, he has been a trailblazer for the host of current rock performers who provide androgynous models for young people—Michael Jackson, Prince, Culture Club's Boy George, Annie Lennox, Motley Crue, Howard Devoto, and Steve Strange.

Not to be outdone by the music world, television has gotten into the gender-blender act with NBC's made-for-TV movie *Her Life as a Man.* This movie and others like it have sex reversal as the main theme.

People magazine contends that "nowhere is gender blending more obvious than in women's fashions."[16] And no less a fashion watchdog than *Vogue* reports, "On the streets from New York's East Village to London's Kensington High Street, boys and girls, men and women sift through the same clothing racks in the cities' 'hottest boutiques.' "[17]

Giora Dilibeto writes:

> Designer Calvin Klein has hit pay dirt with a line of women's lingerie modeled after men's undershirts and jockey shorts. Calvin's 100-percent cotton undies come in six varieties of tops, eight types of bottoms and 25 colors. The bikini briefs are cut high on the leg, but the string bikini resembles a jockstrap and the boxer shorts actually have a fly.[18]

Klein's underwear line is expected to gross $70 million in its first fourteen months on the market.

24

CULTURE IN CRISIS

All this is not just a phenomenon invented by designers, hair stylists, or even rock stars. Gender blending is a real part of the culture. In fact, some see it as prophetic of sex roles of the future.

Writer Jan Morris (her name was James Morris before her operation) ponders the possibility that humanity is "on the road to intersex; perhaps the world of today, by some inexplicable perception, sees characters like Boy George and me as examples of its own sexual future."[19]

While Morris's observation is more wishful thinking than reality, one thing is clear: The blending of gender is far more than a passing fad on society's most bizarre edge. Those of us who still think otherwise are sadly mistaken. Unisex is gaining acceptance in mainstream America.

At the 1984 Grammy Award presentation, "a worldwide television audience of 65 million witnessed Eurythmic singer Annie Lennox's stunning impersonation of Elvis Presley. Then Culture Club's vocalist, Boy George, dressed in a vampish black satin gown, thanked America for knowing a 'good drag queen when it saw one.' "[20]

Future Shock author Alvin Toffler sees far more serious implications in the confusion of sexual roles. In *The Third Wave* he writes:

> The role system that held industrial civilization together is in crisis. This we see most dramatically in the struggle to redefine sex roles. In the women's movement, in the demands for the legalization of homosexuality, in the spread of unisex fashions, we see *a continual blurring of traditional expectations for the sexes.*[21]

"This society wide crack-up of the role structure upon which industrialism depended," adds Toffler, "is far more revolutionary in its implications than all the overtly political

25

protests and marches by which headline writers measure change."[22]

Toffler maintains that the breakup of the traditional role structure through gender blending is one of several factors that "produce crisis in that most elemental and fragile of structures: the personality." Victims of that personality crisis are described by Toffler as anxious "to become what they are not. They work to change jobs, spouses, roles and responsibilities."[23]

And why shouldn't they? When something as basic as one's sexual identity can be changed at the drop of a hat, everything else is up for grabs, too.

We march down the road to homogenized sexual identity at great personal and corporate peril. Even the sacred image of God as the Father has not escaped the eroding influence of the gender blenders. The Inclusive Language Lectionary Committee of the National Council of Churches is attempting to create a nonsexist language about God.

> When it came down to actual titles for God, the committee pulled out all the stops. "Son of God" became "Child of God," "Lord" became "Sovereign One," "Son of Man" became "Human One," and "King" and "Kingdom of God" turned into "Monarch," and "Realm of God" respectively. The most controversial alteration—even within the National Council of Churches—was the change from "God the Father," to "God the Father [and Mother]," or at times, "[God my Mother and] Father."[24]

A national unisex mentality must necessarily be preceded by the destruction of sexual identities. The accompanying emasculation of the American male will not bring about equality. Rather, it will cause further confusion and ultimately lead to the destruction of the American man and his family.

WHICH WAY TO MANHOOD?

There can be no doubt—the modern American male is suffering from an identity crisis of monumental proportions. False icons of masculinity have risen to fill the vacuum created by his loss of his sense of manhood.

The image of the macho maniac calls men to unobtainable heights of strength and courage while it strips them of all human sensitivity. It is an icon of a warrior without a soul.

The image of the great pretender beckons men to mask their fearful ignorance with a facade of macho verbiage. It is an icon of a living lie.

The image of the wimp pleads with men to surrender. It begs them to avoid conflict at any cost. It is the icon of a coward.

The image of the gender blender invites men to trade their masculinity for the identity of unisex. It calls on them to pervert creation. It is an icon of masculine suicide.

These are not the only phony icons of masculinity, of course. There is the superjock, in whom athletic ability is falsely equated with masculinity. There is the comedian who hides his true self behind an endless stream of jokes and pranks. And there is the little tycoon, who falsely equates masculinity with financial security and insulates himself from family and friends in a manipulative world of high finance and stockholders' meetings. But each of these images is just as inappropriate a model of manhood as the others. Following them has done great harm to the American male.

Men need to look elsewhere for something more, and I believe they can find something more by turning back to the not-too-distant past.

3

WHEN MANHOOD CAME TO AMERICA

Both society and household were frankly patriarchal in the seventeenth century.

Mary Ryan[1]

The men who first arrived on America's shores had very little resemblance to the predominant male images of today. If they had, they would never have dared to cross the Atlantic in the first place. Our addresses would still be the cities of London, Edinburgh, and Paris.

COLONISTS AND POLITICIANS

The first foot to step on American soil for the purpose of establishing a permanent English settlement belonged to a man. In fact, all of the 105 settlers who established the initial settlement at Jamestown in 1607 were male. From the beginning, men were the leaders of colonial society. Even when women came to the New World, men maintained control of politics, economics, theology, and family life. Did the women resent their role? We will look at that question shortly.

A prominent historian of colonial society, Mary Ryan, states that early American men assumed oversight of the

28

household: "Only the patriarch of the family . . . could rise to leadership in political, cultural, and religious affairs."[2]

The colonial political world was a man's world. When the first representative political body in the colonies, Virginia's House of Burgesses, was established in 1619, it provided that all *men* over the age of seventeen could vote to elect their officials. In the following year, men alone comprised the forty-one signers of the Mayflower Compact governing the Pilgrims. Such political domination by men was typical in the colonial era.

THEOLOGY: A MANLY TOPIC

As with politics, theology in colonial America was the domain of men. "Men ruled the church as they did the state. Men dominated theology."[3]

Unlike some men today who "delegate" their religious responsibilities and moral duties to women, the colonial man considered spiritual leadership in the family to be of primary importance. Dad was the one who decided matters concerning the religious upbringing of the family's children.

Even the colonial courts did not tamper with the father's prerogative to be the religious instructor of his children. Edmund S. Morgan in *Virginians at Home* writes:

In 1708 Ann Walker, an Anglican married to a Quaker, objected in court to having her children educated as Quakers, but the Court, while acknowledging her own freedom to worship as she chose, instructed her not to interfere in any way with the instruction of her children, even forbidding her to expound any part of the scriptures to the children without her husband's consent. Such complete support for the husband's authority is all the more remarkable in view of the fact that the Anglican Church was the established church of Virginia, to which all the members of the court doubtless belonged.[4]

29

Men governed the church as well as religious affairs in the home. Within mainstream churches, both Puritan and Anglican, only men assumed the principal leadership roles. Peter Stearns states, "Patriarchal Christianity was of course a man's religion. Men were its principal priests. Men were not only the leading but the most numerous church members in societies such as seventeenth-century New England."[5]

Theology was the most popularly discussed topic in the marketplace as well; it was even more popular than politics. Professor Ann Douglas of Columbia University writes, "Until roughly 1820, this theological tradition was a chief, perhaps the chief, vehicle of intellectual and cultural activity in American life."[6] Colonial men made theology an important part of their lives. It was not just for the clergy. How many men today are, in practice, the spiritual leaders they ought to be?

There was no tolerance for heresy. Sin was openly exposed and evil boldly confronted. Discussions in pastoral get-togethers resembled the New Testament account of the heated debates over circumcision at the Jerusalem council; the don't-intimidate-or-challenge-anyone conversations held in ministerial associations today are nothing like that. Colonial men were not shy about the prospect of entering into intense doctrinal discussions. They sharpened their faith by courageous public debate. It was part of being a man!

By contrast, I heard of a pastor who visited a neighboring pastor, and in the course of their conversation, he bemoaned the shameful divisions that exist within Christendom. The neighboring pastor replied that such was not always the case. He noted that for over half its life the church was united in the essentials of the faith—common doctrine, common worship, and common government. He proceeded to suggest that the pastors of the area get together and address the critical issues that divided them.

"Oh!" said his visitor. "It would not be good to discuss doctrine among ourselves. Doctrine divides! We need to stay away from controversy and just get to know one another through prayer."

Needless to say, the churches in that community have continued to be divided. Why? Because prayer is never a substitute for solid New Testament debate and instruction.

Sometimes I think pastors head the pack of those who have fallen victims to the feminizing processes of our American culture. Their view of the Christian faith, rather than being biblical and historical, is shaped by a twentieth-century sociotherapeutic mentality. They've become Reverend Relational, Father Flimsy, and Pastor Passive.

Granted, men of the cloth need to be caring and sensitive. But not to the ridiculous point of saying that everyone is right. They dare not compromise the desperate need to struggle over real issues of belief by hiding under a misuse of words like *love* and *prayer*. True masculinity allows for testing and debate, even within the church.

The church urgently needs to return to the ways of our spiritual forefathers and be willing to view once again the critical role of doctrinal debate as a part of true masculinity.

FAMILY MATTERS

As with the church, colonial families were also unquestionably overseen by men. It was a paternal society. Like Abraham, Isaac, and Jacob of old, colonial men held to the patriarchal model of family structure. "Both society and household were frankly patriarchal in the seventeenth century based on the supreme authority of men as fathers," writes professor of history Mary Ryan. "Women were subject to fathers and husbands within the household, and barred from positions of independence and authority outside it."[7]

Whether a wife lived in a luxurious mansion or a one-room cabin, she was legally subject to her husband's authority. Edmund Morgan informs us:

31

A married woman, so far as the law was concerned, existed only in her husband. If he died before she did, she was entitled to a life interest in a third of his property, but during his lifetime, he had the use of all of her real property and absolute possession of all her personal property. He even owned the clothes on her back and might bequeath them in his will.[8]

And unlike today, when 90 percent of the children in single-parent homes live under the mother's direction, the colonial father had charge of the children. Morgan continues, "He had the right to order the lives of her children, even to the point of giving directions in his will for their management after his death."[9]

Any authority that a woman exercised—and sometimes her power *was* considerable—was always carried out under the blessing of her husband. She was a capable, industrious, and integral part of family and economic life, but she never functioned independently of her husband. Her intent was always to cooperate with his leadership.

At home, in the marketplace, in the statehouse, and at church, men occupied the positions of ultimate headship.

CHAOS OR CONTENTMENT?

This poor colonial creature! How could she take it? She must have been depressed, frustrated, and terribly lonely. Under the unquestioned rule of a frontier patriarch, lacking the advantages and conveniences of modern technology, she was also excluded from positions of ultimate power in political, economic, religious, and family life. The colonial wife must have been utterly miserable and downtrodden!

But she wasn't! Not by a long shot, history tells us. Comparisons show that the colonial woman rarely suffered from the most common problems plaguing the anxiety-ridden woman of today. And the reason, I believe, this colonial

woman fared better than her twentieth-century sister was because the colonial man knew who he was.

Colonial men had a high view of women and did not regard
their position of headship as license to abuse their wives. The
predominant view of marriage among colonial men was that
it was

> to be managed so by the Husband, as that his Wife may take
> delight in it, and not account it as Slavery, but a Liberty and
> Privilege. . . . He ought not, under pretense of Authority, to for-
> get that she is the nearest Companion that he hath in the
> World, and is his second *Self*. . . . It was his duty to love his wife,
> to be patient with her, and to prove himself worthy of his posi-
> tion by being a good provider and a wise counselor. The wife,
> on the other hand, owed her husband deference, but not slavish
> obedience. Both respect and common Interest oblige her care-
> fully to Consult him in every matter of weight, but she could
> always debate the Prudence of the thing.[10]

Today, both men and women are deceived into thinking that
a husband's authoritative manliness is a detriment to the
well-being of a wife. Colonial history proves otherwise. True
manhood produces not only productive women but contented
women, as a comparison of the colonial family with the
twentieth-century family will show.

To help guard my objectivity, I have called upon the careful
labors of a number of scholars. Though I find myself in some
disagreement with the conclusions of these academics, I am
indebted to their insight and work.

As a result of their efforts to find an accurate history of the
American woman, these scholars have also unveiled much of
the neglected history of the American male. And one of their
strongly implied conclusions is that women of colonial times
did far better in their relationships with men than women
have done since that period of time. The reason this is so important can best be shown by the results of a survey conducted by noted psychologist and best-selling author Dr.

James Dobson. He conducted a survey of ten thousand American women, asking them to list their sources of depression. Do you know what? The four primary sources of depression they listed were almost completely unknown to their colonial sisters! What were the most commonly listed sources? Low self-esteem, fatigue and time pressures, loneliness, and absence of romance in marriage.

1. The Problem of Low Self-Esteem

Dobson writes,

Believe it or not, *low self-esteem* was indicated as *the* most troubling problem by the majority of the women completing the questionnaire. More than 50 percent of the group marked this item above every other alternative on the list, and 80 percent placed it in the top five. This finding is perfectly consistent with my own observations and expectations.[11]

But low self-esteem didn't seem to be a problem for the colonial woman. Mary Ryan, after explaining how women were excluded from "institutions of ultimate economic authority," makes the following ironic observation: "Yet colonial daughters, mothers, and wives were unlikely to feel useless or alienated from their labors. The subsistence economy did not eviscerate the female personality by inhibiting women from dealing directly with the material world and battling with nature to serve human needs."[12]

Ryan notes further: "A [colonial] woman's sense of self-worth found solid confirmation day in and day out as her labors contributed to the prosperity of her family and the good order of society."[13] Lacking the consumer mentality that plagues many modern American women, the colonial woman herself was productive, and she felt absolutely essential to the care and maintenance of the colonial family. Since economic order was kept by the colonial male, it was up to him to manage the family in such a way that each woman knew she was indispensable. The patriarchal husband not only provided the context within which his wife could share in the economic stability of the family but also offered her the blessings and praise she deserved. The colonial woman didn't suffer from low self-esteem.

2. The Problem of Fatigue and Time Pressures

The second most common source of female depression identified in Dr. Dobson's survey was fatigue and time pressures.

How did the colonial woman, who had an average of eight children, made most of the family's clothes, cared for the cattle and processed the milk products into butter and cheese, bred and fed the poultry, cared for the family garden, butchered the livestock, bartered her spare products in the marketplace, taught her children—and did it all without automobiles, electricity, or running water—survive with fewer complaints about fatigue and time pressures than the woman of today?

She knew how to spell relief! The patriarchal arrangement carried built-in assistance from the extended family. Grandparents usually lived in the same house or often next door. They weren't divorced from assisting in the hands-on care and nurture of their grandchildren. Yes, the colonial woman suffered from a higher rate of maternal death because of the lack of medical assistance, but there is no evidence that she died from being overworked. Grandparents, young single women, aunts, and other members of the extended family relieved the young colonial mother, especially with the care of the children. No drop-your-kid-off-with-total-strangers daycare centers for these mothers.

Remember, it was *because of,* not *in spite of,* patriarchy and the extended family it produced that the colonial woman was offered more assistance with the burdens of daily family life than her modern counterpart.

3. The Problem of Loneliness

The third and fourth most common sources of depression, in Dobson's study, finished in a dead heat. They were (3) a sense of loneliness, isolation, and boredom and (4) the absence of romantic love in marriage. Says Dobson: "I doubt if there is a marriage counselor alive who has gone through a single day of his practice without hearing about these twin complaints."[14]

Once again, the life of the colonial woman stands in stark contrast to that of today's lonely and unloved woman. "Although women's position at the center of the little commonwealth rendered privacy and the luxury of solitude almost impossible, it also banished loneliness, claustrophobia, and insulation from the essential operations of society," writes Professor Ryan. "In the social sphere, as well as in matters of economics, the women of the seventeenth century enjoyed integral participation in community life."[15]

4. The Problem of Absence of Romance in Marriage

Like loneliness, the absence of romantic love in modern marriage suggests that countless American women desire more expression of love from their spouses. But such has not always been the case. Indications are that romance was a vital part of the colonist's married life. Take, for example, this excerpt from a poem by Anne Bradstreet who, in the mid-seventeenth century, wrote to her husband:

If ever two were one, then surely we.
If ever man were loved by wife, then thee.
If ever wife was happy in a man
Compare with me, ye women, if you can.
I prize thy love more than whole mines of gold,

Or all the riches that the East can hold.
My love is such that rivers cannot quench,
Nor aught but love from thee give recompense.
Thy love is such I can no way repay;
The heavens reward thee manifold I pray.[16]

And such expressions of love were not the exclusive domain of women. Women could express themselves as Anne Bradstreet did only when their love was reciprocated by colonial men.
Listen to Ryan again:

> When early Americans spoke of love they were not withdrawing into a female byway of human experience. Domestic affection, like sex and economics, was not segregated into male and female spheres. Woman's love was expressed in active interchange with her marital partner. It did not precede marriage but grew out of the day-to-day cooperation, sharing, and closeness of the diversified home economy. The reciprocal ideal of conjugal love thrived in the social and economic sphere where men and women were integrally associated.[17]

Colonial men were not the tyrants that some would expect to find in a patriarchal society. Nor were men the unfeeling macho or repressed Archie Bunker types of today. They were real men, unafraid to express their love for their spouses.

> We have many such correspondences between husbands and wives in colonial New England which reveal a degree of intimacy, a respect for each other's minds and spirits, and a delight in each other's company that are seldom to be found earlier, and that by the mid-nineteenth century have become rare indeed.[18]

Among the eighteenth-century letters that have been preserved are many that passed between husbands and wives. They reveal much warmth and tenderness. Theodorick Bland, absent with the American armies in New Jersey in the winter of 1777, wrote to his wife:

37

For God's sake, my dear, when you are writing, write of nothing
but yourself, or at least exhaust that dear, ever dear subject
before you make a transition to another; tell me of your going
to bed, of your rising, of the hour you breakfast, dine, sup, visit,
tell me of anything, but leave me not in doubt about your
health. . . . Fear not, my Patsy—yes, "you will again feel your
husband's lips flowing with love and affectionate warmth."
Heaven never means to separate two who love so well, so soon;
and if it does, with what transport shall we meet in heaven?[19]

While some colonial men were undoubtedly self-conscious,
Bland's expressions of affection, which could only come from
a man at peace with his masculinity, is far more common
than such confidence among modern males.

FATHERS AND SONS

According to Jay Kesler, president of Taylor University,
"The identity crisis of today's young people, individually and
corporately, is the largest single factor affecting this generation."[20] So how about the boys of colonial America? How did
they fare under patriarchal fathers?

There is no evidence that colonial youths were plagued by
questions of who they were. Since colonial fathers were sure
about their roles as men, they could pass on confidence and
security to male youths. In fact, the way in which gender identity developed in America is a noteworthy study in itself.

Instead of perceiving babies as boys or girls, colonial parents and society viewed them simply as "babies." That is why
in the early years, while the children were primarily under
the mother's care and nurture, it was fairly common for boys
and girls to wear identical clothing. Many of us may recall
visiting Aunt Susie and seeing baby pictures of Great-grandpa
wearing dresses. Boys and girls were cared for in much the
same way until the age of five or six.

Then, at about age seven or eight, a big change took place

for a boy. He was taken from the primary care of his mother and brought under the direct supervision and instruction of his father. The boy would be almost constantly at his father's side. He would learn to work and act like his father and even dress like him.

By contrast, young boys of today constantly change their dress to fit the latest fads. Their models are their peers or slightly older boys. At an early age our sons start wondering whom they are to be like. The option of an endless line of "pop" heroes or styles of dress and behavior was not open to colonial boys. Their models were set, their identity secured. They knew who they were.

Identity came more from being linked to a family than from being just an individual. A young man was "the Jones boy," and he knew where he belonged and what he was to be.

Further, a young colonial boy knew his contributions to the family's success secured *his* future interests as well. This made for a direct, meaningful connection between him and his father. This relationship helped to ensure proper behavior on the part of the son; it was clearly understood that he would receive his father's property only after he had proved himself obedient.

The colonial father also taught his son how to be coura- geous. The long, hard work on the farm and the adventures of hunting for food for the table gave plenty of opportunities for the boy to increase his stamina and to take needed risks as he learned to do his tasks. Every father held in his mind the vi- sion of preparing his son to face the wilderness. It was filled with perils and foes, both human and animal. Even the weather provided hardships that had to be endured with courage and tireless strength. An early ballad called "Fore- father's Song," written about 1630, has two lines that reflect this call to courage:

> But you whom the Lord intends hither to bring,
> Forsake not the honey for fear of the sting.[21]

39

The boy learned at an early age that pain was not an enemy to be avoided at all costs. The colonial father no doubt gave more room for his son to develop male characteristics than the boy's mother would have allowed. The normal wrestling and rowdiness of young males were tolerated as training and testing for the beginnings of manhood.

Colonial life was vigorous. Teen-age males of that time had to handle work responsibilities that only adults face in modern America, but they had been trained to handle those responsibilities. Colonial boys could cope.

DATING AND MATING

There are, however, some pressures of today the colonial youth did not have to bear. One of the most prominent of these is the current pressure of premature "pairing off." Few facets of modern life weigh as heavily on our young people as the modern dating system. Tremendous force is placed on teens, by their peers and the culture as a whole, to "pair off" before they are emotionally ready to marry.

Sociologists tell us that our enlightened modern approach to dating has produced an epidemic of child parents, kids who are depressed (many to the point of suicide) because of repeated romantic rejection, and youths who will one day change marriage partners with the same frequency with which they now change adolescent sweethearts.

Such bad fruit of modern dating practices was seldom experienced by colonial youths. Why? Because colonial fathers protected their sons and daughters from unilateral decisions surrounding courtship. Colonial youths did not pair off unless they were seriously pursuing matrimony. There was little recreational dating. And even then, they did so only with the blessing and guidance of their parents.

Typical of the attitudes and practices of colonial times are those seen in this letter that Eliza Southgate wrote to her parents about Walter Bowne:

> He knew I was not at liberty to encourage his addresses without the approbation of my Parents, and appeared as solicitous that I should act with strict propriety as one of my most disinterested friends. . . . He only required that I would not discourage his addresses till he had an opportunity of making known to my Parents his character and wishes. . . . That I feel deeply interested in Mr. Bowne I candidly acknowledge, and from the knowledge I have of his heart and character I think him better calculated to promote my happiness than any person I have yet seen. . . . I have referred him wholly to you, and you, my dearest Parents, must decide.[22]

Such a dating-and-mating system based on parental approval might appear extremely rigid, but this ancient tradition was a major reason the colonists produced healthier marriages than our current fool-around-and-choose-your-own-and-probably-not-make-it routine. The colonial dating system with its paternal oversight worked, as Eliza, who received her parents' permission to marry Mr. Bowne, later testified, "I realize all the happiness that you can wish me."[23]

EXTENDED FAMILIES

As in ancient times, patriarchy also guaranteed the historical continuity of the extended family for the colonist. One particular man was responsible to see that all the family members lived in geographic proximity to one another and cooperated with one another to the benefit of all. His job was to rule in such a way that peace and unity were maintained. This extended family was made up of grandparents, parents, uncles, aunts, cousins, children, singles, and in-laws. Everyone belonged. Everyone was important to the welfare of the family.

Grandparents were involved in extended families. They

41

weren't viewed as useless to the family or as old people to be entertained only on holidays. Nor did they retreat from family life by constantly indulging in the "pleasure" of cruising America's trailer camps in their motor homes.

With old age came dignity. Instead of practicing the cultish worship of youth we see today, society most respected men and women who had lived long on this earth. And the wisdom gained by living many years was considered a great asset to the entire family structure. When the extended family collapsed, Grandpa and Grandma were no longer considered a vital part of the family unit.

Single adults also suffered when the extended family collapsed. In colonial times they didn't encounter the kinds of problems facing their twentieth-century counterparts.

Contrary to the separationist identity of today's independent single, being single in the seventeenth-century meant serving within a household structure. The economic and emotional support system of the single was secured, and the individual's self-esteem was bolstered by the vital role played in helping the entire extended family prosper.

Sadly, when the extended family shattered with the fading role of the father, single adults were not considered part of the new concept of the family. They were forced to develop their own peers, activities, and independent status, which set them quite apart from the norm of history.

First Grandpa and Grandma were displaced, then single adults. And to this day, the boundaries of the household have continued to shrink. We are left with a new definition of the family described by social forecaster John Naisbitt in his number one best seller, *Megatrends*:

> Today's family can be a single parent (male or female) with one or more children, a two-career couple with no children, a female breadwinner with child and househusband, or a blended family that consists of a previously married couple and a combination of children from those two previous mar-

riages. Although conservative family groups vehemently object, the term *family* is being expanded to include important relationships between people not related by blood or marriage, but by voluntary association: unmarried couples, close friends or roommates with long-standing relationships, group houses where people living together have grown into a community.

But what is even more basic is the way the family, or at least the household, consists of only one individual.[24]

Historical family relationships have disintegrated. People have become islands to themselves. Loneliness is rampant. Unity is becoming a myth as we see the extended family, and now even the nuclear family, collapsing under the weight of selfish individualism. America's preoccupation with independence and individual fulfillment has left men, women, and children estranged from one another.

I am not suggesting that we plow up the pavement and tear down the apartment buildings of twentieth-century urban America. Or that we should trade in our cars for oxen, our washing machines for scrub boards, and our condos for isolated country cabins. Not at all. But I am suggesting that the colonial man has some very important things to teach the man of today. It was *because of*, and not *in spite of*, the patriarchal constitution of the colonial family that its members did so well. But soon would come far-reaching events that would lead to a dramatic reshaping of American manhood— the Industrial Revolution and the Second Great Awakening would lead to a new spirit of independence.

4

FROM PATRIARCH TO PATRIOT

To reject authority became a praiseworthy and specifically American act . . . the making of an American
demanded that the father should be rejected both
as a model and as a source of authority.

G. Gorer[1]

With the passion that only a preacher could muster, he tri-
umphantly proclaimed that America's struggle for independence from Britain would "begin a new era in the annals of
mankind, and produce a revolution more important, perhaps,
than any that has happened in human affairs."[2]

These visionary words are from the prophetic pen of Dr.
Richard Price. A highly valued friend of both Benjamin
Franklin and John Adams, Price gave incomparable aid to the
Revolution through the political essays he wrote and distrib-
uted throughout England.

Dr. Price probably didn't realize that this new era he envi-
sioned would not only revolutionize the political situation in
America but would also inadvertently alter and even damage
the role of the American male.

But before I go on to develop this point, let me take time out
for a moment. I love our nation and am thankful for the benefits of living in this country. I have never failed to exercise my
duty to vote. I've gone door to door campaigning for presiden-

tial candidates. I was an enlistee in the U.S. Army. I would willingly die to defend this nation, and I would let my only son give his life in defense of her if need be. I love the flag. I even venerate the flagpole! But this one thing I know. If men are ever to regain what they have lost, they must acknowledge that there is a fly in the ointment of the American Revolution. In addition to political freedom, the Revolution also gave birth to a spirit that would ultimately be the undoing of the American male: the spirit of independence.

THE PRICE OF REVOLUTION

The Revolution was born out of an admirable desire to shrug off unjust British rule. But as often happens, the baby was thrown out with the bath water. In this case, the baby was the essential paternal pulse of colonial life. Instead of correctly identifying and trying to escape from *oppressive* patriarchalism, Americans began to look upon *all* civil patriarchy as inherently evil, and they became intent on not being ruled by anyone. In a later essay Dr. Price gleefully described America as "a rising empire, extended over an immense continent, without bishops, without nobles, and without kings."[3]

That may all sound quite liberating, but it was an idea unprecedented in the history of humanity. There have *always* been bishops and kings and accountability. The development (and growing acceptance) of the idea that patriarchy is evil must have had a jarring effect on people with a Christian heritage. Up to that time, Christians had been taught to "honor the king" because earthly kings represented the "King of kings," and godly bishops imaged "the Shepherd and Bishop of their souls." How in heaven's name could this new anti-authoritarian attitude be reconciled with such biblical injunctions?

The independent spirit that energized Price's vision soon permeated every aspect of American life. Independence was

45

all but enshrined as a national virtue. As it spilled over into economic, religious, and domestic relationships, it began to profoundly alter our concept of manhood. The same bell that sounded forth for political liberty in the colonies rang out a death knell for American fatherhood. Aided by the Industrial Revolution and the Second Great Awakening, thousands of years of responsible manhood crumbled into a pile of rubble—all in less than a century.

This new unquenchable thirst for independence created new heroic models for the men of the late eighteenth and the nineteenth centuries; these models took the place of the colonial man, who was courageously devoted to the welfare of his family. These men were the epitome of strength, determination, and courage, to be sure. But, tragically, they were also the essence of independence. And they were sorry examples of patriarchs.

Davy Crockett was married three times.[4] The adventurous Simon Kenton of frontier fame would disappear into the wilderness for months at a time without a word to his wife about when he was departing or when he planned to return. On one occasion, after being gone from home too long, Daniel Boone returned to discover his wife had just given birth to his brother's son![5]

Historian Peter Stearns tells us of this era: "The male heroes were unflinching captains of industry, the warriors, the frontiersmen, or even the two-fisted missionaries."[6] Were free-spirited men like these the actual forerunners of our current macho men who can't uphold family life?

INDEPENDENCE GOES TO CHURCH

This new revolution of independence, as social cancers always seem to do, finally affected the church as well. Self-ordained men, appointed and sent out by no one, began to ride west with Bibles tucked under their arms to join the swelling ranks of wandering frontiersmen. We are still haunted by this image of the *E Pluribus Me* independent frontier preacher, who rides into town again in our time in films such as Clint Eastwood's *Pale Rider.* "Preacher," as Clint was called, was really just a gunslinger in clerical garb. In time, many of these colorful but independent preachers unwittingly helped sanctify and legitimize the thoroughly secular virtue of independence and helped give birth to a distinctly novel American anomaly, the independent church.

An already divided Christendom began to fracture even further. Almost two thousand years of Christian consensus on the essentials of the faith was spurned as independent churches produced independent members who came up with independent interpretations of the Scriptures. The proliferation of modern and very independent cults tells us the rest of the story.

This legacy of independence among Christians remains, of course, a prominent feature of modern American Christianity. Yet it seriously bothers some who fear its consequences. I can remember sitting in the office of a prominent leader of a large international parachurch ministry not too many years ago and hearing him admit, "I hate the use of the name 'Independent Church.' It arrogantly declares a blatant unaccountability to the rest of the body of Christ." I could not escape the undeniable truth of his statement.

The rise of clergy who were connected to nobody would cost many Americans dearly. If authority tends to corrupt, and absolute authority corrupts absolutely, let it be clear that unaccountability corrupts, and absolute unaccountability corrupts even more so! The concept of private biblical interpretation opened wide the door to every conceivable heresy. Recall that the Mormons' Joseph Smith, the Jehovah's Witnesses' Charles Taze Russell, and the Christian Scientists' Mary Baker Eddy all claimed full belief in the Bible. But they all—in the spirit of their day—insisted upon their own independent interpretations.

. . . AND THE HOME

But it was not just the religious folk who were influenced by national independence. The American family took its lumps, too.

In 1776, just three months before the Declaration of Independence was signed, future First Lady Abigail Adams wrote to her husband John,

> I long to hear that you have declared an independency. . . . And, by the way, in the new code of laws which I suppose it will be necessary for you to make, I desire you would remember the ladies and be more generous and favorable to them than your ancestors. Do not put such unlimited power into the hands of the husbands. Remember, all men would be tyrants if they could. If particular attention is not paid to the ladies, we are determined to foment a rebellion, and will not hold ourselves bound by any laws in which we have no voice or representation.[7]

If men had gained their independence from authority, why couldn't women have theirs, too? That only seemed fair. Thus, the changing roles of men *and* women began at the very birth of our country. Even there, forces were starting to stir, forces that would drastically alter family life for everyone: wives would question the rule of husbands; sons and daughters would rebel against the authority of parents; grandchildren would challenge the wisdom of grandparents.

The same independent spirit that sent colonists to war with Britain would put family members at odds with one another. As Lawrence Fuchs observes, "With its emphasis on personal independence and equality, American ideology is at war with the very nature of family life, at least as it has been known through the ages."[8]

. . . AND THE ECONOMY

The independence movement was also fueled by dramatic economic changes. Like a bomb, the Industrial Revolution burst upon the scene. Colonialism had survived with the common productive unit of rural household industry. However, by 1815 American household productivity was well on its way to being demolished and replaced by industries located outside the home. The evolution of industry would be a powerful catalyst of the continued growth of the independent nation.

The colonial period had ended. American leadership realized that industrialization was an indispensable ally of independence. Thus, Ann Douglas notes, "Jefferson, once the staunch defender of agrarian life, explained in 1816 that 'experience has taught me . . . manufacturers are now as necessary to our independence as to our comfort.' "[9]

Soon the homespun woolen industry, once a part of most every colonial home, became virtually extinct because of the overwhelming presence of twelve hundred cotton factories in the United States. The death of this home trade was typical of the way that factories replaced home industry.

FROM FARM TO FACTORY

What did industrialization do to the American family? Because no profit could be made by producing goods at home, people began to work at the factory. When the doors opened wide to the first large mechanized factories at the close of the eighteenth century, women and children, as well as men, entered through them en masse. A textile firm in Rhode Island was the first to adapt to mass production techniques that created the need for hiring a large body of laborers. This company's owner "recruited families as his labor supply, removing entire households from farm to factory." In fact, this new industry provided employment to women and children in such great numbers that "by 1816, a report on the United States cotton industry listed 66,000 women operatives, 24,000 boys, and only 10,000 adult men."[10]

Although women had always been essential to the economic survival of the household, they had never before directly competed with men. Before this time, men had their own distinct spheres of work on the farm. While they worked in close cooperation with their wives, they never had identical jobs. Not until now.

With men and women sharing identical jobs at the factory, their roles became confused. Men sought new ways to preserve their masculinity. The first distinction to arise was economic—women would earn less than half what men were paid. In addition, women would be given the more menial jobs.

But even these differentiations did not eliminate competitive feelings between men and women. Something more drastic and radical had to be done to regain the clear distinction of the male role. The idea of the man as the sole breadwinner for his entire family was born. This change represented an entirely new line of economic thinking for men.

One cannot fathom what a major turn of events was taking place at this time in American history. Although many women continued to work in industry, the aim of men was to send women back home—and back to the home they went. As a result, the woman's increased presence in and the man's increased absence from the home would be the major cause of the woman's becoming the new "practical head" of the family. Peter Stearns writes,

> The same division of labor that made the man breadwinner outside the home gave the wife increasing control of the family. A man might seek and claim dominance, but he simply was not present for day-to-day decisions ranging from allocation of money to raising of children. Patriarchalism in this situation

would be rather hollow, though man and wife both might, for their own reasons, pay lip service to it.[11]

Interestingly enough, during the Industrial Revolution when the American male traded in his role as paternal manager of the household economy for the new role as sole economic supporter of the family, he became dependent on a whole new system. "The household economy was clearly no longer autonomous," writes Mary Ryan, "but increasingly dependent on relations with other enterprises and reliant on money and credit to meet its needs."[12]

This dramatic transition literally jolted the role of men in America. Once farmers, and the children of farmers, these men exchanged work around their homes and families for new occupations in factories. And in most cases, this new situation required men to leave their homes for long periods of time. Men began to lose their grip on who they were.

Commuting became a new difficulty. A man couldn't hop in his BMW and drive forty-five miles in forty-five minutes; twenty-five miles was an all-day journey. Numerous men left their families in the rural areas while they worked in the bustling cities. Others, who lived close to their jobs, put in such long, toilsome hours each day that it became almost impossible for them to provide the normal care that fathers had previously given so carefully to each member of the family. There was no longer time or energy.

FATHERS AND SONS

Other problems began to surface. When Dad left the farm for the factory, he no longer had land, cultivated for several generations, to pass on to his son. Tensions began to mount. "Patriarchalism was severely affected," comments Stearns. "A propertyless worker might rage at his son, try to dominate him physically, but the vital hold was gone. The son could walk out without great damage to his economic future."[13]

51

Young people became free from patriarchal and community control. For all practical purposes, American fatherhood was dead. The resulting confusion of the male role and the confused state of masculine identity produced an incredibly high level of stress in men that caused them, for the first time, to die sooner than women. As Stearns notes, "It was in the nineteenth century that women began to outlive men in the Western world."[14]

The American male, at this crossroads in history, suffered greatly as he lost his place and his role as personal guide and leader of his family on a day-to-day basis. And much of the time that he once gave to the affairs of the family would be devoted to the role of being an employee in an impersonal factory atmosphere.

So the Industrial Revolution disconnected men from home life. No longer looking to their patriarchal function in the family as the focal point of their male identity, men were forced to seek new alternatives for passageways to manhood. And it didn't take young men long to exchange the old passageways for the new. Sociologist Peter Stearns confirms that three popular rites of passage soon dominated the national scene: getting into fistfights, drinking booze, and having sex outside a marital relationship.[15]

The working-class male proved his masculinity by engaging in one, two, or all three of these activities, and his reckless pursuits brought cheers of approval from fellow factory workers. It was at this time that the number of tavern owners skyrocketed and prostitution flourished. New York City authorities estimated that between 1200 and 7000 prostitutes roamed the city streets early in the nineteenth century.

Because sexual conquest became a new male attribute, young men experimented sexually at a much earlier age, resulting in another new problem: the rise of illegitimate births from 1780 onward.

Fighting, drinking, and engaging in sex, of course, are still

the primary means by which hordes of American males secure their pseudomanly roles.

A CHANGE IN NATIONAL CONSCIENCE

The next fatal blow against the paternal order of the family,
and against fatherhood itself, came in a rather unexpected
and subtle way when the state added more social pressure by
removing the encouragement of religion in public life. American leaders helped undo the manly mixture of politics and
religion by new declarations of independence from the provi-
dence of their Creator.

In the preface to his "Defence of the American Constitution," written January 1, 1787, John Adams, the future president of the United States, boldly dismissed the idea of man's
dependence upon God to providentially guide him in "the
land of promise," by saying,

> The United States of America have exhibited, perhaps, the first
> example of governments erected on the simple principles of
> nature. . . . Thirteen governments thus founded on the natural
> authority of the people alone, without a pretense of miracle or
> mystery. . . . The experiment is made, and has completely suc-
> ceeded.[16]

God was being expelled from the affairs of government.
In time, according to Ann Douglas,

> the Protestant Church in this country was gradually trans-
> formed from a traditional institution which claimed with cer-
> tain real justification to be a guide and leader to the American
> nation to an influential ad hoc organization which obtained its
> power largely by taking cues from the non-ecclesiastical cul-
> ture on which it was dependent.[17]

This pressure to officially disengage the Christian faith
from public life did not go unnoticed by many of the clergy of
the day, either. "Lyman Beecher [1775–1863]," Douglas con-

tinues, "a prominent Congregational clergyman, preaching fervently against the imminent disestablishment of the Connecticut church in 1812, predicted grimly if extravagantly that, under its dispensation, 'we shall become slaves, and slaves to the worst masters.' "[18]

Whether we agree with what developed or not, politics triumphed over Christian theology. A new god, rational humanism, emerged. " 'Your own reason,' Thomas Jefferson once wrote to a nephew, 'is the only oracle given you by heaven.' "[19]

When the state pulled the rug out from under the church, men no longer identified being Christian with being masculine. After the state's dismissal of Christianity in public affairs, men felt personally inhibited to discuss theology in the marketplace. Christian commitment was thoroughly divorced from masculinity.

Taking their cue from the state, individual men began to forsake God and take up the pursuit of the materialistic promises of the Industrial Revolution, commonly called the "American Dream." Theology was replaced not only by politics but also by commerce as the hot topic among men in the marketplace. It was no longer manly to talk about religion.

As men left the church and ceased to discuss theology, the American view of God would now change as well. It was at this time, according to Stearns, that "the image of God lost ground."[20] American Christianity now began to focus almost exclusively on a feminine and sentimental Jesus. This would have an increasingly negative effect on American men.

With the Father in heaven missing from view, the father in the home took a leave of absence as well. How? With theology depopularized, men, for the first time in American history, began a mass exodus from the church. Stearns says very pointedly that "Exposed to a competitive, acquisitive economic world and, often, to a secular education, many men lost an active religious sense. Male recruitment to the clergy declined. In many villages, and even more in working-class communities, regular church attendance was left to women."[21]

By the early 1800s, the majority of the Christian faithful in America were women.[22] And not only were women the most numerous members; in time, they came to dominate the spiritual attitudes of the church.

WOMEN: FROM PRODUCERS TO CONSUMERS

To understand why this change came about, we turn to take a closer look at the effect the Industrial Revolution had on women. When men became sole economic supporters of the family, women were deprived of their former role as producers and became, instead, consumers. Their new task was to keep the home fires burning.

However, it was not just the home fires that burned. Women as consumers began to burn holes in their pocketbooks as well. One writer comments that the Industrial Revolution swallowed up the family enterprise and "drew the head of the family and his trade from home, leaving his wife alone with the children in a more secluded and monotonous household, no longer his partner but an economic parasite."[23]

By 1830, writes Ann Douglas, "middle-class women were far more interested in the purchase of clothing than the making of cloth." Everything had changed for women at home. "Domesticity itself is altered beyond recognition; women no longer marry to help their husbands get a living, but to help them spend their income."[24]

Unlike their mothers, who oversaw and directed the busy, productive processes of the home economy, many of these new industrial middle-class women, "having nothing to do, or choosing to do nothing of a useful nature, found time heavy on their hands."[25]

This domestic shift received attention from at least one

man, the prominent president of Yale University, Timothy Dwight, who wrote,

> Women of this description crowd to the theatre, the assembly-room, the card-table, routs, and squeezes; flutter from door to door on ceremonious visits, and from shop to shop to purchase what they do not want, and to look at what they do not intend to purchase; hurry to watering places, to recover health which they have not lost; and hurry back again in search of pleasure which they cannot find.[26]

This, of course, was thankfully not the case with all women. But the general consensus of American historians is that women in the early to middle 1800s began to feel worthless, bored, and trapped in their homes, holding a new sense of consumerist guilt. They were women without a cause.

But not for long!

FINNEY AND THE SECOND GREAT AWAKENING

Women got religion. The Second Great Awakening was born. This was not the first time American women had been stirred by a spirit of revivalism. Both men and women had been involved in the First Great Awakening during the mid-eighteenth century. But a major change in revivalism would profoundly influence the country in the early nineteenth century.

"These revivals do not appear to have involved a cross section of the population," writes historian Barbara Epstein. "Ministers wrote that converts were usually young, most often between the ages of fifteen and twenty-five, either single or married but without children, and predominantly female."[27]

Not only were women the most numerous converts of revivalism, but in time, they became its most vocal proponents.

According to a study by Epstein, "among the forty-seven male converts whose accounts have been examined in this study, sixteen mentioned the influence of religious women in their families; the rest did not mention their families or spoke of them only in passing. None of the women mentioned the influence of men in their families."[28]

Women also dominated the organizations spawned by revivalism. In *The Origins of Modern Feminism* Jane Rendall says,

> Women's associations multiplied rapidly. Prayer groups, mission societies, benevolent reform societies, Sunday School organizations: all clearly derived from the revivalist movement. The large cities and small towns of New England all had their own, spontaneously generated, local associations.[29]

Displaced in her role as an essential producing component of family industry by the Industrial Revolution, the American woman found in revivalism, among other things, a new place to employ her energies. Rendall states, "The appeal of such movements to women was immense, both because of their fitness for women's qualities, and because, as Harriet Martineau said, 'women pursued religion as an occupation.'"[30]

But the new flood of female religious activity was not a leaderless phenomenon. It was a response to the call of dynamic, powerful leadership. The grand spokesman of revivalism came suddenly on the scene in 1824. Born in 1792, Charles Grandison Finney was an "independence baby." In his day, Finney became the most well-known evangelist born this side of the American Revolution. He would introduce a new, individualistic style of revivalism that would affect believers for generations to come.

Finney was an attorney by profession, a man who was adept at powerful persuasion. As to his theological training,

> he was mostly self-educated in religion, which he largely ignored until his thirtieth year and then clasped possessively. He

crammed in enough private study to be ordained by the Presby-
terians, but in effect he always remained a layman. Never having sat at the feet of scholars in divinity as a youth, *Finney had
no hesitation about writing his own doctrinal platform in a
bold script.*[31] (Italics mine.)

Ignoring the historical tradition of interpreting Holy Scripture within the consensus of the church, Finney boldly paved
the way for independent biblical interpretation. As recorded
in *They Gathered at the River*, "Finney leaned more and more
heavily on the Bible as he interpreted it. . . . For enlighten-
ment on hard questions, the aggressive soul-winner said, he
could go 'directly to the Bible, and to the philosophy and
workings of my own mind as revealed in consciousness.' "[32]

This same bold revivalist preacher, who strode dramatically across the stage conspicuously dressed as an attorney
rather than in traditional clergy garb, would unwittingly become a father of modern feminism!

Finney skillfully made use of middle-class women who
were ripe for a cause. His message and style were particularly effective at reaching the female heart; rather than
emphasize manly characteristics, such as courage, ag-
gressiveness, and a desire for justice, Finney aimed toward
the feelings and emotions of the potential convert. As a result,
many more women than men responded to his message of revival.

In the Finney revivals, both men and women were called
upon to pray aloud. This marked a radical break with the
practice of a lot of people who, up to this point, had taken the
instruction of Saint Paul for women to be quiet in the church
quite literally. In fact, women were expected to express themselves both in public meetings and in small groups. Because
of this open involvement of women, the evangelist Finney
soon found himself opposed by the rest of the clergy of the
day. A paper written in 1823 on female influence by the Pres-

byterian Utica Tract Society called Finney to task for placing women in unbiblical roles in relationship to men.

This opposition led Finney to defend himself by traveling to upper New York State as a representative of the Utica Female Missionary Society. Finney's staunch support of female involvement resulted in the emotionally charged Utica awakening where women poured into the revival movement to sign up for missionary endeavors. Finney was on a roll. He had tapped into a resource that would change not only the society at hand but the whole nature of the American Protestant church.

Sidestepping the apostle Peter's admonition that wives should win their husbands by conduct rather than words, the evangelist encouraged women to begin their verbal crusade at home. He warned, "I have known women who felt they ought to talk to their unconverted husbands, and pray with them, but they have neglected it, and so they get into the dark. They knew their duty and refused to do it; they went around it, and there they lost the spirit of prayer."[33]

This strategy for winning the husbands at home was backed up by the organization of women's neighborhood prayer meetings. In Bath, Maine, a minister wrote that "in a certain neighborhood, all the wives were persons of piety. These females were given to prayer. For this purpose they met together. Their husbands were always the subjects of prayer."[34]

This tactic apparently had some success. Charles Finney enthusiastically welcomed the triumphant testimonies of those faithful wives who succeeded in winning the souls of their wayward husbands. One such woman dramatically caught the attention of the famous revivalist who recalled that "there appeared in her face a holy joy that words cannot express."[35]

Do I deplore the conversion of husbands and fathers? Absolutely not! But in the flurry and emotion of revivalism, the

59

vacuum of spiritual leadership that was created when men deserted the church was filled by women. With their deep concern for the souls of their husbands, Christian women inadvertently took upon themselves the responsibility that biblically and historically had been carried by men: being the spiritual head of the home. One minister told of a woman who converted in the course of a revival meeting: "The first exhortation she gave was, as she flung herself upon the neck of her husband—an unconverted man—'O, my dear husband, you must submit, you must submit.' "[36]

During the Second Great Awakening, men began to return to the church. But when they did, it was under the spiritual matriarchy of their wives. Men's subordination to the force of feminine spirituality greatly alarmed some of the clergy. "A minister who opposed the revival in his town wrote that as a result of it 'there are many men, who begin to doubt whether they hold that place in their houses, and in the affection and regard of their wives and daughters, which, by nature, by law and by gospel, belongs to them.' "[37]

The female leadership and dominance in the Finney revivals were overwhelming. Whenever he spoke in towns and cities throughout this nation, women rose to his cause. Not only were women called to be evangelistic in the home, but the call came for them to hit the streets as well. It was at this time that women began to use outreach endeavors as opportunities to organize for moral reform. Historian Jane Rendell notes,

> The work of Finney was a major element in this change, since in his revivals from 1829 onwards, Finney called upon New Yorkers to go through the streets seeking converts. The number of tract distributors, male and female, grew tenfold from 50 at first to 500 in 1830, and in his second revival, from 1834–5, over 1000 laymen and women were engaged in this work. The relevance of this was to lie in its direct impact on female organization. In the spring of 1834 a group of New York

women, under Finney's inspiration, founded the New York Female Moral Reform Society.[38]

The women of America were openly challenged to be the leaders in bringing virtue and purity to all spheres of society.

The clergy began to pick up on the feminine drum roll. Women were the majority of their congregations because of the revivals, and pastors gradually gave way to this swelling tide. One minister, capitalizing on this new phenomenon, exhorted his female members:

> We look to you, ladies, to raise the standard of character in our own sex; we look to you to guard and fortify those barriers, which still exist in society, against the encroachments of impudence and licentiousness. We look to you for the continuance of domestic purity, for the revival of domestic religion, for the increase of our charities and for the support of what remains of religion in our private habits and publick institutions.[39]

Women had religious authority, and they would develop political clout as well. "It is not surprising that many of the women who were touched by God in Finney's revivals became the feminist leaders in the nineteenth century," writes evangelical Kari Malcolm.[40]

Women, displaced by the Industrial Revolution and hungry for purpose, picked up through the vehicle of revivalism the mantle of headship in the home dropped by men when they left the home and the church for the factory. The men of the mid-1800s looked nothing like the colonial patriarchs.

A MIXED HERITAGE

True to the biblical declaration, the sins of the fathers have passed on from generation to generation. The problem of the fragmented family and the social and moral chaos surrounding us today have sprung forth from seeds of idolatrous independence planted as long ago as the American Revolution.

61

Our forefathers, in their search for freedom, forsook patri-archal responsibilities in church and in society. They dele-gated their spiritual duties to women, they walked out of the church, and they lost sight of God as Father. In their haste to grab the gusto of the new Industrial Revolution, they em-braced the ancient lie that life consists more of what you own than what you are. Men today are surrounded by incredible technological toys, but privately they are a wrecking yard of broken homes and of moral corrosion.

5

VICTORIA'S SECRETS

"The ladies will do nothing until the gentlemen of the audience leave the house." And the men adjourned to "leave this work with God and the women."
Colonel Isaac Trimble[1]

Carry Nation was the daughter of an insane mother who believed she was Queen Victoria. The wife of a Campbellite Christian preacher, Carry publicly ridiculed her husband for his weakness of speech until he finally left her. Likening herself to the apostle Paul, Mrs. Nation bore the self-proclaimed messianic title of "Defender of the Home" in nineteenth-century America.

Carry could whip her devotees into an instant frenzy. She was the local general who called women to holy war against the consumption of alcoholic drink. "Take your consecrated hatchets, rocks and brick-bats, and everything that comes handy," she told them, "and you can clean this curse out! Don't wait for the ballots! Smash! Smash!"[2]

Thousands of women throughout the country enthusiastically responded to the battle cry of this Woman's Christian Temperance Union (WCTU) activist. Tormented by visions day and night, Carry Nation struggled violently, she believed, with Satan himself as she smashed up the saloons of America while the WCTU cheered her on.

63

What incredible irony! The Judeo-Christian patriarchy that had once witnessed Jesus Christ, the Son of man, cleaning out the temple with a whip had sunk to the humiliating low of a pathetic, crazed Victorian woman cleaning out the taverns of the land with a rusty axe. Thousands upon thousands of women converged upon these sanctuaries of fraternalism in America and literally reduced them to splinters while the men just stood by and watched! (Rightly or wrongly, the local tavern was one of the few remaining places men could go to be in the company of other men.)

After Carry Nation and three female companions demolished his tavern, James Burnes was asked by an astonished bystander, " 'Why didn't you knock the woman down?' 'God forbid,' said Mr. Burnes, chivalrously, 'that I should strike a woman.' Within fifteen minutes the four women had wrecked the saloon with a thoroughness that would have done credit to a cyclone."[3]

Why didn't the men resist, through the civil authorities, the courts, the National Guard? They didn't *dare* resist. This was the age of the reign of the Victorian woman. By the time these incidents occurred, new values for American culture had been set firmly in place for over half a century. Women had become the moral directors of society. During this period of history, American women came to believe that "the influence of woman is not circumscribed by the narrow limits of the domestick circle. She controls the destiny of every community, the character of society depends as much on the fiat of woman as the temperature of the country on the influence of the sun."[4]

This is the critical period of national history from which most American men have never recovered. During the Age of Victoria, roles in crucial areas of social life were dramatically reversed. The Victorian period, by its very name, symbolizes feminine domination. The unofficial national emblem was an all-sovereign matriarch, Queen Victoria of England.

The side effects of independence and the new time demands of commerce caused the boat of masculinity to take on water. But instead of bailing the water out and making repairs, men chose to jump ship. They made a deliberate decision to create new roles for themselves and their wives that would excuse them from the responsibilities of moral guidance for home and society. Men saddled women almost exclusively with the burden of being the collective moral conscience of America.

For the first time, moral leadership and courageous acts of benevolence would no longer be viewed by America as masculine attributes. They would become women's work. For all practical purposes, men officially excommunicated themselves from the three most important spheres of social influence: the home, the school, and the church.

A new gender system was created to validate that exile. American men sold their patriarchal birthright for a life of banishment to the island of politics and commerce. They copped out, exchanging true masculinity for a shallow, imitation manhood that would deteriorate into a futile sense of worthlessness and confusion. And this blurring of Victorian male identity has produced a twentieth-century male who is more troubled about his manhood than his counterparts in any other time in American history.

STEPS IN THE PROCESS

As a pastor, I have spent countless hours with families who suffer under the grandsons of these Victorian men—husbands and fathers who have withdrawn into their workaday worlds. They are men who refuse to take responsibility. Their passivity and inaction affirm that spiritual leadership in their homes belongs to their wives. They are bankrupt men who dramatize their plight by dropping their wives and children off at church during the football season and signal their sons that the spiritual world is for women and children.

How did these new Victorian roles become the norm of the day? I have identified five steps that I think had a significant part in this process.

Step One: The Presence of the Pedestal

If men were going to withdraw as the moral directors of society, others needed to fill the vacuum created by their retreat. Men did not want to get rid of all moral influence. They just wanted to shed the final *responsibility* for morality. And they found just the candidates for the job—Victorian women. So women, who were always equal in value to men in the eyes of God, were artificially elevated to a position of moral supremacy over men. This is the famed "pedestal" of the Victorian era.

The women of the nineteenth century were extremely vulnerable. Once dynamic and essential parts of the family's economic survival, women had shamefully been displaced by industrialization. Because they had been removed from the role of producer and relegated to that of consumer, their dignity suffered greatly. They were ready for a cause, and the trip to the top of the Victorian pedestal set them on a course that would have a tremendous impact on American society.

Partly because of time demands and the emergence of new priorities created by their obsession with the world of commerce, and partly to compensate disestablished women, men created a new "doctrine of spheres." Men would rule the workplace, and women would rule the home—and all the other spheres of moral influence including the school and the church. To justify this radical new concept, Victorian men erected a whole new gender system: They not only abandoned their roles, but purposefully and systematically divorced themselves from virtually every meaningful area of moral responsibility. Men ruled politics and commerce. Women ruled everything else. The seeds of modern feminism were beginning to sprout.

As Queen Victoria powerfully reigned over England (and the rest of her empire), so would her American sisters rule over the hearts and minds of American men. At least that was the ideal. What an incredible paradox: The grandsons of men who rejected the reign of kings were to be ruled by a host of queens.

As Mary Ryan observes,'

> Invested with love and gentleness (not energy or power), women were suited to reign only in the domestic circle, on "the throne of the heart." From their little kingdoms, however, women were assured that they could dictate national morality, preside over the tone of American culture as surely as Victoria reigned in England.[5]

Hear me out: It was not the fault of the women. American men were the chief architects of the fantasy of Victorian feminism. There she stood, the Victorian woman regally perched on her pedestal with her pinched waist, swelled bosom, and layers of petticoats atop her hooped skirt. Rarely soiling her tender hands by physical labor inside or outside the home, this new "lady" filled her days with strolling about or reading sentimental fiction and, of course, the Holy Bible, of which she had become the sole guardian. How could it be different? In the mind of the Victorian man, she had become "a gentle household divinity . . . the source and sacred fountain of our happiness."[6]

The nineteenth-century American man looked upon this woman as a veritable domestic goddess who ensured an environment of purity for the offspring and the holy conscience for an entire nation. In contrast to the aggressive businessman or the unrefined factory worker, she was the embodiment of beauty and virtue. As Myron Brenton has written, "She was glorified. She was idealized. Her virtues were praised to the skies, and of faults she was deemed to have none."[7]

Although no woman could fully achieve the ideal, this Victorian image was the goal to be pursued by the entire female population of America. Her exploits were dramatized and exaggerated in a flood of sentimental novels written by women, for women. Her virtues were even praised in pulpits across the nation, and her flowing words of civil piety were etched into the plaques that graced the walls of every Victorian home. This female mystique overwhelmed even the male heroes of the day.

Step Two: The Moral Surrender of Men

The creation of this all-moral superwoman came at tremendous cost to the Victorian man. He would pay dearly. The price for her inauguration would be his emasculation and feminization. Why? Because when he so cowardly bowed at the foot of the Victorian pedestal, he surrendered himself to be a moral number two to the opposite sex.

Throughout history, men had been the moral examples and teachers for their families. But due to the male cop-out, women replaced men in these roles, and they "set their menfolk an example of superior moral excellence."[8] Women were "increasingly assumed to be potentially closer to God. The prescriptive literature of the period emphasizes that latent moral superiority."[9]

This new view of men and women permeated the entire nation through a flood of books and magazines that constantly reinforced the moral supremacy of women.

The mainstay of the national publishing industry was books for, about, and by women. For the first time in American history the topic of womanhood was among the central preoccupations of the national culture and had been standardized to obliterate local and regional variations. By the 1850s female readers were imbibing directives in femininity through the vicarious experience of sentimental novels.[10]

An avalanche of Victorian literature was aimed primarily at women. Why? Women, not men, were the readers who were seeking to educate themselves for the new role of moral leader. That trend has not changed even to this day. This very book you are reading, written by a man, will most likely be read by more women than men. Women age twenty-five to forty-five account for 70 percent of book purchases. This twentieth-century phenomenon is so pervasive that the majority of current books about manhood are authored by women.

From 1820 to 1860, book sales increased from $500,000 to $12,500,000.[11] Victorian literature was essentially used to develop the superiority of women. Most of the literature endorsed the new gender images by depicting men who were almost totally dependent on women for moral guidance.

Step Three: The Active Control by Women of Home, School, and Church

The stage was set. The actors were in place. As sociologist Peter Stearns says, "The role was, finally, new: Women had never before been granted moral supremacy."[12]

The first realm that men surrendered to the benevolent rule of their newly crowned moral superiors was the domain of the once-patriarchal home. Since the founding of America, as we have noted earlier, men had been the possessors of household authority. But with patriarchal responsibilities increasingly replaced by the demands of industrialization, men of the Victorian era were away from home far too much to properly maintain their historical function. Stearns agrees: "A patriarchal approach to the family was one key to keep it separate from the competitive quality of the business world. Yet because the economic struggle was so demanding, businessmen lacked the time to extend patriarchal control over every aspect of the family operation."[13]

In addition, men were beginning to see that the values of the marketplace often conflicted with the values a father should want to instill in his family members. Stearns continues, "It was not a question of time alone. Many businessmen realized that they were consumed by a market mentality which, while fully justified, was not appropriate as the moral basis of the family."[14]

Materialistic Victorian men found themselves faced by a dilemma. At work, competition was the key value; at home, cooperation was esteemed. In the factory, the personal welfare of workers was less important than making a profit; at home, nothing was more important than the welfare of the family members.

The problems were very real. Men had no time left for their families. What were they to do? How were they to provide leadership? Simple! They had their wives do it. Rather than attempt to restructure the workplace in a way that would allow them to maintain their patriarchal duties, men restructured the home by practically deserting it.

The groundwork for the twentieth-century fatherless home was set. For the first time, it was socially and morally acceptable for men *not* to be involved with their families. Before the close of the nineteenth century, notes Lawrence Fuchs in *Family Matters,*

An Englishman observed that while his countrymen were continually going home, American men were continually going to business. At home the American male was sometimes a playmate, occasionally a nullity, less and less an authority. It was at work that he usually made his presence and power felt. In 1912 a writer in a Paris newspaper asserted what other Europeans had been saying and thinking for generations: While the American man rules in the business world, his wife rules at home.[15]

While some trappings and patriarchal symbols remained as reminders of the past, the real power in the Victorian home shifted from men to women.

> The wife, so well endowed with grace, intuition and a ready emotional sympathy, has as her mission to preside over the internal life of the house, whose well-being she ensures by her knowledge of domestic details. The man may take great pride in providing for the home, but would there be anything distinctly manly about being in it, now that it was his wife's domain?[16]

Not hardly. True acts of manhood vanished when men abandoned their fatherly involvement with the family. And men had to come up with new acts in an attempt to preserve their identity as men. No longer able to relate in a normal role, men began to take on new and strange roles, such as the macho man, the great pretender and, most frequently, the American wimp. Of the nineteenth century, Professor Ryan writes, "Observers of one middle-class neighborhood described the husbands of the district as a goaded, henpecked, and spineless crew."[17]

Women soon discovered that while this "transformation" of American children began at home, it was brought to maturity at school. And they also discovered that the key to the kingdom of the home, given to them by men, also unlocked the door of the school.

This predominant feminine influence upon America's children was applauded by the leading educators of the day. Horace Mann, the greatest liberal educational reformer of his time, was one of the first to experiment with free co-educational public schools and the mass training and recruitment of teachers. Who were these teachers? Increasingly, they were the women of America. "As public schools rapidly spread across the land in the wake of the Horace Mann experiments in Massachusetts, an army of women was trained to

71

staff them. By 1890 there were 244,342 female teachers in the public schools, as compared with 124,449 male teachers."[18] Women controlled the newly formed classrooms of the public schools. As they did, men were displaced as the educators of America's children. Another male responsibility down the drain!

As a child, I attended an elementary school named after the renowned Horace Mann. The army of women he unleashed seemed to dominate this school as well. From my recollections, the only men were the principal and the janitor. This has been a fairly common situation since over 83 percent of elementary teachers are women.[19]

What is the significance of this educational history? During the Victorian era, irresponsible men dumped on the women of America the sole responsibility for two of the most powerful institutions for shaping the character of future generations—the home and the school. Men might retain some administrative control over these spheres, but feminine thoughts would personally and intimately form the actions and reactions of American children.

The increasing absence of male influence from the home and the school has made it more difficult for each succeeding generation of young males to be secure in their masculine identity. For in female-dominated homes and classrooms "boys are exposed to the continuous authority and teaching of agents whom they may not imitate, but whose guidance and information about what they should be they are expected to accept and practice."[20]

What's really frightening is that homes and schools are even more dominated by women today than they were during the Victorian era. This female rule was strikingly portrayed on the front cover of the September 20, 1985, edition of *Christianity Today*. The feature story illustrated on the cover dealt with issues of home and school tensions. And what symbols did *Christianity Today* choose to portray these two American institutions? Believe me, there wasn't a man in sight. The exasperated parent and the frustrated teacher were both—you guessed it—women.

The home and the school were not the only spheres of influence vacated by the men of America during the Victorian era. The third, and most critical, domain over which Victorian men submitted to women was the Protestant Sunday school. In fact, women so completely dominated the Protestant churches that the feminized character of the churches became obvious. Nancy Cott writes, "The 'feminization' of Protestantism in the early nineteenth century was conspicuous. Women flocked into churches and into church-related organizations, repopulating religious institutions."[21]

As the church became feminized, ministers felt obliged to appeal openly to women to guard the home and even society at large from the moral bankruptcy of men. Early in the nineteenth century, Rev. Joseph Buckminster called upon his female parishioners

> to raise the standard of character in our own sex; we look to you, to guard and fortify those barriers, which still exist in society, against the encroachments of impudence and licentiousness. We look to you for the continuance of domestick purity, for the revival of domestick religion, for the increase of our charities, and the support of what remains of religion in our private habits and publick institutions.[22]

By their own hand, men became spiritually dependent upon women. Peter Stearns observes, "Not surprisingly, religious imagery stressing the woman as latter-day Eve, properly subordinate for her sin, yielded to that of woman as redeemed and pure, to whom more worldly men were urged to look for their own spiritual guidance."[23]

I cannot begin to relate how many women I have heard over the years talking about the need for their husbands to be the spiritual leaders of the home. Then to my surprise, when their husbands began to take that responsibility, many of these same women resented it. Why? Because when men begin to establish spiritual leadership, they threaten women's role of moral supremacy. Women have been schooled in Victorian thought, and to them, losing the spiritual leadership in the home also means losing control in the raising of the children.

This female domination of the religious and moral upbringing of children continues to this day. A 1984 *Gallup Report* on religion in America informs us that "the stronger influence on the average teen's religious and moral upbringing comes, by a very wide margin, from the mother. Nationally, fully 59% said their mother had exerted the strongest religious and moral influence, while only 16% named their fathers and 20% gave both parents equal credit."[24]

This female spiritual rule rears its head in subtle ways. How many family gatherings have you attended at which Aunt Ivy or some other spiritual matriarch gathered the relatives for a word of prayer or devotion before the meal began? And how many times, when a man has prayed, has he done so only at the beckoning of the spiritually sensitive woman who "submissively" asked, "Dear, isn't it time to pray?" as if he could never think of it without her reminder?

Some years ago, I went to a conference at a beautiful, remote Christian retreat center in Oregon. The dining room was filled with about thirty pastors, along with the camp director and his wife. Who gathered us in a circle, had us hold hands and sing a song I hadn't heard since Sunday school, and then led us in prayer?

If you guessed it was one of the pastors, you're wrong. If you guessed it was the camp director, you're wrong, also. I'm sure the camp director's wife is a fine woman but, obviously, like the Victorian woman, she is one who has no qualms about assuming a position of spiritual leadership—even at an all-male retreat. And our male silence implied that it was all right for her to do so. A modern tradition has been established.

Since the nineteenth century, men have, in reality if not in words, abdicated the spiritual headship of their families to women. Victorianism saw spirituality crowned feminine. Women were seen as the last great bastion of the Christian faith. One Protestant minister said, "I believe that if Christianity should be compelled to flee from the mansions of the great, the academies of the philosophers, the halls of legislators, or the throngs of busy men, we would find her last and purest retreat with women at the fireside; her last altar would be the female heart."[25]

The most prominent place in the church where the power of feminine influence was demonstrated was the Protestant Sunday school.

> The opening and proliferation of Sunday Schools dramatized the ministerial and feminine struggle for possession of sacred territory. Sabbath Schools, begun in England in the later eighteenth century as a means of educating, and controlling lower-class children, spread rapidly in America in the early nineteenth century. In 1817–18 the Sunday School Union had forty-three schools and 5,970 pupils: a scant six years later, it could boast 723 schools and 49,619 pupils. From its inception, the Union was funded largely by businessmen, but the most active promoters and organizers were ministers and women.[26]

The Victorian mold is even more firmly established in most Protestant churches today than it was in the nineteenth century. Women, not men, are sitting in the teacher's seat. This lack of male input is high on the list of what many young boys dislike about Sunday school. I don't say that they hate women, but that they hate a feminized system that belittles their attempts to be masculine.

When Victorian men gave the Sunday schools to women, that was only a part of the great spiritual giveaway. Even in such socially conservative denominations as the Southern Baptists,

> women were doing much of the work by the end of the century. They were the teachers in most of the Sunday School classes (except adult male classes), they were conducting most of the benevolent work of the churches, and they were promoting the mission program of the churches with very little assistance from the men.[27]

Step Four: The Elevation of Motherhood over Fatherhood

With the shift in roles, Victorian theology as well as philosophy openly declared motherhood more important than, not equal with, fatherhood. Feminist historian Nancy Cott notes,

> Ministers fervently reiterated their consensus that mothers were more important than fathers in forming "the tastes, sentiments, and habits of children," and more effective in instructing them. Their emphasis departed from (and undermined) the patriarchal family ideal in which the mother, while entrusted with the physical care of her children, left their religious, moral, and intellectual guidance to her husband.[28]

So great was this new influence upon the American culture that in 1833, educator V. S. C. Abbott wrote in his work, *The Principles of Maternal Duty,* that "mothers have as powerful an influence over the welfare of future generations as all other earthly causes combined."[29]

It was because of this Victorian mind-set that Mother's Day was officially recognized by the U.S. Congress in 1914 as a national observance. But the American obsession with Mother made itself felt throughout the year. It should come as no surprise that a day honoring fathers, while observed by some, did not become an *official* American observance until over half a century later.

This preoccupation with Mother has never left us. We are

reminded of it in the most subtle ways. Consider, for example, the twentieth-century phenomenon that regularly takes place upon the television screen when the camera zooms in and selects the hero from a college or professional sporting event. Does he ever wave his hand and say, "Hi, Dad?" No way! In forty years, I've never seen it happen. The American jock always says, "Hi, Mom!" In fact, this is so noticeable that America's well-known comedian, Bill Cosby, has done an entire routine about this odd development.

When men gave women control of children in once male-ruled spheres, they set the stage for even greater feminine dominance in society at large. The Victorian woman, whom men enthroned as the moral savior of the home, school, and church, expanded her domain to the poor, the disabled, and the helpless members of society.

Step Five: Responsibility for Public Mercy and Moral Reform Goes to Women

It had always been a mark of manhood to care for the poor, the orphan, the widow, and the stranger. But male involvement in these areas all but disappeared in the Victorian era.

"Once the civic duty of town fathers and poormasters, subsequently the charge of the welfare state, the care of dependent populations was known as charity in the nineteenth century, and became the province of women."[30] The new Victorian gender images of men as hard and self-absorbed and of women as calming and benevolent set the philosophical stage for the abdication of male responsibility.

Not too far into the nineteenth century, female charity and reform societies abounded, especially in the industrialized cities. Professor Ryan writes,

The larger cities offered women sufficient benevolent activity around which to build a full-time career. A young Boston woman named Susan Huntington, for example, belonged to the Female Orphan Asylum, the Graham Society, the Corban Society, the Female Bible Society, the Widow Society, the Boston Female Education Society, and the Maternal Association. She served as an officer in at least three of these organizations. Thus, by 1830 female charity had become a major component of the urban social system. It would grow more comprehensive and entrenched as time went on.[31]

And who were the debased, wretched scoundrels who needed the reforming touch of these feminine movements? The men, of course. Again Ryan notes,

Almost all the female reform associations were implicit condemnations of males; there was little doubt as to the sex of slave masters, tavern-keepers, drunkards and seducers. One women's crusade, Female Moral Reform, made this assumption explicit and often in a virulent manner. It directed women's ire toward the American male and shouted as its battle cry, "Level your artillery at the head and heart of the debauchee."[32]

Do you see the significance of this change? In less than a century, irresponsible men, having handed over their responsibility to care for the poor, deserted, and outcast souls of society to the "morally superior" women, became the objects of these moral crusades. Since all men were suspected of being innately morally inferior to women, women felt justified in their assault on American masculinity and male vices of every kind. Women have continued to dominate the social conscience movements to this day.

Recently, a female caller on a local talk show asked the radio host, "Why do we never see Fathers Against Drunk Drivers? Why is it always women who carry the burden of these problems? Where are the men?"

The radio host responded, "I don't know."

In the latter part of the nineteenth century, when the people of France wanted to honor the social conscience of Americans who had welcomed oppressed immigrants, they bestowed the honor with the gift of a statue of a woman who compassionately proclaimed with silent lips,

Give me your tired, your poor,
Your huddled masses yearning to breathe free,
The wretched refuse of your teeming shore.
Send these, the homeless, tempest-tost, to me,
I lift my lamp beside the golden door!

This poem on the base of the statue identifies her as the "Mother of Exiles." We know her better as the Statue of Liberty. She was pure Victorian, this grand lady, right down to her pedestal!

Moral strength and generosity are portrayed today, as then, by women. With the prevailing Victorian view that men were morally unsuited for anything but hard-nosed politics and the aggressive world of commerce, I doubt if anyone ever considered that the statue should be anything but a woman. The statue set forth the spirit of the age.

I think it's great, by the way, that the Statue of Liberty has been restored. I, like you, have immigrant ancestors whom she welcomed to our shores. But now that we have finished the noble work of fixing up the Lady, we would be wise to turn our attention to the restoration of the sad state of American manhood.

NOW WHERE?

Several generations of American boys have grown up under a feminized culture, and each generation has been more confused about male identity than its predecessor. I have traced the historical development of the withdrawal of American men from moral leadership in the homes, schools, and churches of our land. There is not an American male today who has escaped the feminizing influence of Victorianism. The Victorian era's doctrine of spheres brought to a new low a manhood already disenfranchised by the spirit of independence and the Industrial Revolution. The American family began to feel the effects of men who were missing from action.

79

A VANISHING BREED

Most American children suffer too much mother and too little father.

Gloria Steinem[1]

The single most devastating factor contributing to the feminizing of American males is the desertion of families by their fathers. Writer Edwin Cole insightfully notes that "the absentee father is the curse of our day."[2] It is a national plague that is reshaping the very foundations of U.S. society.

In 1983, there were more than 5,700,000 households in the United States with no father present. More than 12,700,000 children under the age of eighteen lived with their mother only. Thus, for a variety of reasons, more than one out of five children in America under the age of eighteen has no father at home, a ratio that will rise to one out of four by the end of this decade.[3]

Unsure and frustrated in their roles of husband and father, married men are deserting their families in droves. Of all the tragedies that their fleeing creates, none is more sad than the abandoned child—unless it is the child who is never wanted in the first place.

LOVE HER AND LEAVE THEM

In numbers never before witnessed, men are refusing to take upon themselves the responsibility of being fathers to the children they helped create. During the three-decade period from 1950 to 1980, the annual rate of illegitimate births increased by a staggering 450 percent. The 715,200 children born without official fathers in 1982 represented 19.4 percent of *all* births for that year.[4] This means that almost one out of every five children born in the United States in 1982 had no father at home. They became children of faceless fathers.

Legions of deserted children were fathered by selfish, irresponsible males with unthinking, won't-say-no sex partners, women who never intended to get pregnant. Many of these couples were out to satisfy their passions without thought of consequences. Their intent was usually not parental. Most were seeking only a good time—recreational sex, they call it now. Many of these faceless fathers are teen-age boys who, upon becoming parents, want to be responsible fathers. But they have neither the knowledge nor the means to do so. The statistics are of little help to the resulting unwanted child.

Over the years I've worked with numerous people whose serious problems of hostility can be traced, at least in part, to a latent insecurity they've carried with them for years. The cause of that insecurity? The focus of that hostility? It was the anonymous father who deserted them before they were born.

THE DIVORCE DILEMMA

An even more prevalent cause of missing fathers is the national divorce disgrace. In 1981, the average husband and wife in this country headed to divorce court just seven years after they marched down the aisle. In America, it's likely your dog will be with you longer than your spouse.

There were 1,155,000 divorces granted in the United States in 1984. That's about one divorce for every two marriages performed. Of the 2,487,000 marriages reported in 1982, over 25 percent involved a bride who had been married before.[5] And contrary to the recent glut of articles proclaiming the maturity and stability of remarriage, the hard facts tell a different story. The rate of divorce is *higher* among second marriages than it is among first marriages.[6]

This century, of course, has seen the divorce rate skyrocket. In the last seventy years in America, the annual number of divorces granted has increased by an incredible 1,420 percent! The baby boomers of the fifties have grown up, and in 1985, they were getting divorced at twice the rate of their parents.

And pity the poor kids left behind! To them, having parents go through a divorce is a typical part of growing up. Consider this report: "More than 1,000,000 youngsters a year live through the shocks of a marital breakup. 'Today's children are the first generation in the country's history who think divorce and separation are a normal part of family life,' says sociologist Andrew Cherlin of Johns Hopkins University."[7]

The traumas of divorce are major sources of emotional stress suffered by children. Noted child psychologist and best-selling author Dr. David Elkind says:

We see many more children who show symptoms of stress—headaches, stomachaches, low mood, learning problems. As they get older, many feel that they have missed an important part of their life. They feel used and abused. My concern is that if they don't feel cared about, then they can't ever care about anybody else—or about themselves. We may be creating a large number of children who are emotional misfits.[8]

EVANGELICALISM: THE NEW
FRONTIER IN MARITAL CRISIS

Christians are increasingly becoming a part of these statistics, too. Even though the Scriptures say that God "hates
divorce," Christians are throwing away their marriage commitments at alarming rates.

I remember hearing, not too many years ago, the oft-
repeated claim from the pulpit that the divorce rate among
Christian marriages was low compared to that of the non-
Christian world. I suppose my memory is aided by the fact
that I, too, preached those statistics. But things have changed.
Instead of Christians bearing witness to the secular culture,
that culture has borne witness to Christians. Divorce among
Christians is now gaining rapidly on the national average.

And it's becoming more and more acceptable in larger segments of Christendom. Numerous books tacitly affirming the
state of divorce are popping up at both evangelical and de-
nominational bookstores. Seminars, Bible studies, retreats,
conferences, and "Single Again" Sunday school groupings
are now available to Christian divorced persons. In an attempt to minister to them, we've unwittingly colonized them.
It's as if we're saying, "Hey, it's OK to be divorced."

Most discouraging of all is the disproportionately high rate
of divorce among Christian leaders. The list of well-known
pastors, teachers, evangelists, and writers who have left their
spouses and families is offensive, and it continues to grow. To
my own sorrow, some of these have been close friends.

A few years ago a friend of mine received a telephone call
from a guest speaker at a Christian conference center just a
few miles from where my friend lived. "Would it be all right
for me to stay with your family tonight?" he asked.

"Sure," I replied, "We'd love to have you!"

This man was, and is, one of the most popular speakers in
evangelical circles today. As my friend hung up the phone, he

wondered why this man seemed so eager to spend the night with his family. The conference center had beautiful, comfortable facilities for him, and after all, he was the main speaker.

After they greeted each other, my friend's guest began almost immediately to tell him of the incredible pressures he was under. It was relief from the crowd that he sought. He was booked for hundreds of speaking engagements within that year, was physically deteriorating, and had seen little of his wife and children.

The next day he discussed in some detail the need he felt to change his lifestyle. My friend told about the necessity for all who serve Christ to be accountable to Christian leaders who care enough about them to slow them down. "If I don't get that kind of help," he said, "I'm going to die."

Just two months after that evening, my friend received the tragic news that this man had divorced his wife, left his family, and remarried. So far as anyone can tell, he never missed a beat on the Christian circuit.

Christian and non-Christian alike, men are jumping ship. Through the plague of divorce, they are contributing to the pains of sorrow and rejection felt by the fatherless family. What does this epidemic of departure mean? It signals the desperate need to return to true manhood.

Real masculinity involves a willingness to remain committed to loved ones no matter what circumstance arises. The collapse of adequate models of Christian manhood is producing self-absorbed and often cowardly men who bail out when the going gets tough. These men are demolishing their children by their absence.

VISIBLE BUT NOT PRESENT

But wait. There is yet another category of missing dads. It is this largest group of absentee fathers who are hidden from the view of statisticians. They are the ones living at home! They are there, but they are not making contact.

These fellows have minimal communication with their wives and are almost totally oblivious to their children. According to a California school superintendent, "The average American father does not give three minutes per day, but only 35 seconds of undivided attention to his child each day."[9]

In my twenty years of ministry, the most consistent complaint I have heard from Christian wives is that their husbands lack personal contact with them and their children. It is a charge I hear repeated over and over and over again. Fathers are there physically but not emotionally or spiritually.

It is probably fair to say that hundreds of thousands of American men have forsaken their responsibilities toward their families so that they can pursue other interests. For some, it's wealth and possessions. Others have submitted their lives unconditionally to highly competitive industries so that they can climb a status ladder. Their time belongs not to the family but to the corporation.

For other men, it's not status or wealth per se that captivates them, but work itself. They go at it for endless hours. The salesman on the road, the CPA who brings his ledgers home, or the executive who schedules meetings morning, noon, and night—he never seems to stop. The workaholic has nothing left to give his family. Tired of people and conversation, he merely wants to be left alone at home. The next morning he may shower and leave before the family is even awake, and then he shifts into high gear as he pours every ounce of energy he possesses into his job. And lest I sound immune, we pastors can become churchaholics and never know it.

"Regular guys" who punch the timeclock at 8:00 A.M. and 5:00 P.M. are included in this category, too. Some of them stubbornly resent having to listen to tales of family members' daily experiences around the supper table. Such men swap paternal responsibility for personal pleasure. Imagining they have worked harder than their wives, they plop down in front of the TV for the evening. With expertise that comes with careful practice, they learn to tune out their children.

To this man, a wife exists to care for his needs, the house, the children, and the pets—in that order. Instead of viewing his home as a place to love, serve, and lead, he sees it as a place to rest himself, refresh himself, and amuse himself.

COLOR HIM PASSIVE

A book has finally called it—*Passive Men and Wild, Wild Women*.[10] What a title! But it accurately describes the atmosphere of a home where the man does not enter into the life of the family. The passive father snuffs the growth of his entire household.

Where did the passive father learn this *modus operandi*? It is my opinion that he learned it primarily at school. He may have entered kindergarten free and rumble-tumble, but he soon found his classroom actions too rambunctious and his voice far too shrill. In first or second grade, he found that wrestling on the playground and spitting through the fence resulted in lost recess privileges. By fourth grade, he discovered that if his body remained quiet, he could escape into a world of fantasy and receive little adult disapproval. So there he sat—quietly and passively, five days a week, nine months a year—under a dedicated woman teacher who quite innocently enforced schoolgirl rules. She kept maternal—not paternal—order and gave matronly direction to him and his classmates.

He was taught traditional feminine etiquette and social values. "Talk only when asked to talk." "Initiating activity is unacceptable." "Don't try to supervise the activities of others."

Obedience eventually resembled subordination and repression. The only place he could actively engage himself as a young male was on the playground, not in the classroom. Outside, he could be the initiator, there he could test his courage and build camaraderie with other boys. Inside, it was different—a woman's world. Through no fault of the teacher, classroom life prepared him well to be a passive father at home.

Next time you're present with the man of the house, notice if he speaks except when someone asks him a direct question. If he is like most men, he will seldom initiate conversation. His wife, the female figure, keeps order and gives direction in the household environment. She has replaced his grade-school teacher. His children are his classmates he has learned to avoid indoors, and the TV replaces the fantasies that once cruised through his mind's eye to make school bearable. If we take this a step further, the office and the spa have replaced the playground. They provide an environment where he can actively engage himself once again. There he is involved. There he is an initiator. There he takes risks. There he attempts to act like a man.

Mark it well: A tuned-out father, consciously or subconsciously, prefers to watch the six o'clock news rather than speak with his own children. He would rather eat dinner by the glow of a movie on his VCR than join his wife for a romantic dinner. He would rather lose himself in the distant world of "Monday Night Football" than toss a football with his teenage son. Always self-absorbed, he would rather be served than serve the needs of his family.

Listen to a letter I received from the wife of a Christian friend, which tragically expresses the feelings of countless women in America today. I include this with her permission.

The kids are in bed. There's nothing on TV tonight. I ask my husband if he minds if I turn the tube off. He grunts. As I walk to the set my mind is racing. Maybe, just maybe tonight we'll talk. I mean have a conversation that consists of more than my

87

usual question with his mumbled one word answer or, more accurately, no answer at all. Silence—I live in a world with continuous noise but, between him and myself, silence. Please—oh God, let him open up. I initiate (once again; for the thousandth time). My heart pounds—oh how can I word it this time? What can I say that will open the door to just talk? I don't have to have a DEEP MEANINGFUL CONVERSATION. JUST SOMETHING!

As I open my mouth—he gets up and goes to the bedroom. The door closes behind him. The light showing under the door gives way to darkness. So does my hope. I sit alone on the couch. My heart begins to ache. I'm tired of being alone. Hey, I'm married. I have been for years. Why do I sit alone? The sadness undergoes a change slowly—then with increased fervor I get mad. I AM MAD. I'm sick and tired of living with a sissy. A wimp—a coward. You know, he's afraid of me!

Hostile, you say. You better believe it. I'm sick and tired of living in a world of passive men.

My two sons like sports. They're pretty good. They could be a lot better if their Dad would take a little of his precious time and play catch with them. (I'm sorry, catch once a year at the church picnic doesn't quite make the boys into great ball players.) But Dad's too busy. He's at work. He's at the health club. He's riding his four-wheeler. He's working on the car. He's playing golf. He's tired. He's watching a video movie. So who plays catch with my boys? Me. My husband says, "You shouldn't be playing men's sports." So who's going to do it? He *says* he will. But he doesn't. Remember? *He's* too busy. Satisfying himself doing what he likes. So my poor sons have to be second-rate in sports. They could have been good. Really good. Yeah—I'm mad.

My daughter is a teenager. She likes boys. *They* notice her. *They* pay attention to her. She responds. I know what's coming. I try to talk to her. But it's not me she wants. It's Dad. Yeah Dad! If he'd just hug her, notice her, talk to her—just a little— she wouldn't need those boys so much. But no . . . so she turns elsewhere for attention and love. And there's nothing I can do.

A mom isn't enough. Kids need a father. And not just a body, a passive, silent presence.

And here's the killer. My husband's father did the same number on him. Didn't hug him. Didn't take him to anything let alone watch his baseball games. And he HATES his father. Now my husband's doing the same thing. Will our sons grow up passive? Will they be cowards?

God save us from withdrawn fathers. Taking the initiative to actively *lead* the family is a trait of authentic masculinity. Like the father described in this letter, countless American men have been feminized through the acquired passivity that is characteristic of the way they relate to their families.

It's clear that fatherless families are an increasingly common feature of the American culture. Fatherhood is rapidly becoming a lost art, and its loss is threatening the stability of an entire society. Dad's disappearance is exacting a disastrous toll.

THE SONS OF AWOL DADS

Kids without fathers will grow up damaged. Dramatic events can intervene to change this sad scenario, but in all likelihood they won't.

The chilling reality is that children without dads have potential for great harm, not only to themselves, but to others in society as well. For starters, check this "hall of fame" chronicled by author Daniel Amneus:

Few readers will have heard of Richard Lawrence, Charles Guiteau, Leon Czolgosz, John Schrank, or Giuseppe Zangara. These gentlemen were the assassins or attempted assassins of Andrew Jackson, James Garfield, William McKinley, and Theodore Roosevelt, respectively. Some recall the name of Dean Corll, the Houston mass murderer, and everyone recalls that of John Wilkes Booth. Lee Harvey Oswald, James Earl Ray,

Sirhan K. Sirhan, Charles Manson, Andreas Baader, and Lynette Fromme are household words.[11]

These people experienced the extreme but logical end of what can occur when dad disappears, for they all "share an interesting biographical oddity. They all grew up with no fathers in their daily lives."[12]

SHATTERED SONS

Studies show that father-absent sons "tended to have an unrealistic and feminine fantasy picture of what a father was or should be, behaved in a much more dependent manner and reacted submissively and immaturely to peer influence." Such boys will also "have a strong inclination toward depression."[13] More and more often, that depression reaches its ultimate low point.

Americans were shocked by the heartbreaking news of six students who committed suicide in a middle-class Texas town. One of the six boys was a good-looking football player on his high-school team. His mother, in a TV interview, revealed the struggle of her son. She said that in response to her question about his apparent depression, her son told her, "Mom, you don't understand. You don't know what it is like to not have a father."

And it's not just older boys who sense great loss. Dad's disappearance affects his son even at a very early age. James Herzog is a psychiatrist at Children's Hospital Medical Center in Boston. He recently studied seventy-two young children from single-parent homes in suburban Brookline. His conclusion? "Absence of an active father figure was harmful, and most harmful to male toddlers 18 to 24 months old. These children had recurring nightmares about monsters, which Herzog interprets as a sign of displaced aggression and vulnerability."[14]

Boys without fathers are far more likely than any other children to have a run-in with the law. More than 75 percent of the juveniles arrested are boys. Most of them come from broken homes. A juvenile is three times more likely to be a delinquency statistic if that broken home has no father than if it has no mother.[15]

Boys without fathers simply have a tough time growing up into well-adjusted men. I recall the following all too well:

"Just a minute, honey," cried his worried mother. "Let me help you blow your nose. You can hurt yourself if you don't do it right." Although we were only seven years old, I can still picture this incident in my mind and relive the impression it made on me.

This boy lived just a few houses from me in downtown San Jose, California. He was my friend, but not for long, because he was the son of an overprotective mother and a hen-pecked, passive father. Boys with such parents have few friends. Over the years I watched, with a fascinated interest, the development of this young man's life. His mother was a college professor and, as such, ensured the academic skills of her son. But unfortunately, she also guaranteed the shaping of a feminized male who was destined to experience social annihilation.

Sadly, there was almost no masculine activity in which this boy was allowed to participate. He couldn't go to the nearby creek with the rest of us boys because his mother feared he might drown. He was forbidden to ride his bike on the dirt trails that were provided for the neighborhood boys. His mother was determined that her son would be isolated from feeling any pain.

Since he was always scolded if his clothes were dirtied, the guys dubbed him "Mr. Clean." Even though he was big and husky, he was not allowed to enter sand-lot ball games. And playing football, with its inevitable stains and sprains, was out of the question.

So, he filled his time by vicariously participating in sports. He came to resemble a modern computer in his ability to spit out names and statistics for any player and team in professional football or baseball. After high-school graduation, this walking sports computer went to college on a four-year academic scholarship, but he lasted just one semester.

Being unable to cope within the reality of the student social world and feeling the rejection of his peers, this overprotected feminized male suffered a mental collapse from which he has never recovered. Constantly sedated, this son of a passive father now lives in a pitiful social exile under, of course, a woman's care.

DADS AND DAUGHTERS

Though boys suffer to a far greater degree from father-absence than do girls, who at least have a role model of the same sex present, not having a man around the house affects daughters as well as sons.

Girls have a much more difficult time developing a positive image about themselves when their father is not around. Consider the pain expressed by a high-school senior:

> Have you ever heard of a father who won't talk to his daughter? My father doesn't seem to know I'm alive. In my whole life he has never said he loves me or given me a goodnight kiss unless I asked him to.
>
> I think the reason he ignores me is because I'm so boring. I look at my friends and think, "If I were funny like Jill or a superbrain like Sandy or even outrageous and punk like Tasha, he would put down his paper and be fascinated."
>
> I play the recorder, and for the past three years, I've been a soloist in the fall concert at school. Mom comes to the concerts, but Dad never does. This year, I'm a senior, so it's his last chance. I'd give anything to look out into the audience and see him there. But who am I kidding? It will never happen.[16]

The lack of attention from her dad led this poor girl to the conclusion that she was dull, unintelligent, and all-around boring. Hardly what you'd call positive self-esteem.

Masculine fathers are also a main source from which girls develop their image of femininity. Without the warmth and affection from a present father, young girls begin dating and pairing off at a much earlier age. They become desperate for male attention and approval.

I recall from my high-school years that the most vulnerable girls were those without fathers. They were the ones the boys picked out to "put the make on." Lacking the natural affection and protection a father provides at home, such girls responded eagerly to almost any male who showed them gestures of kindness. Innocent as these girls might have been, they usually fell into sexual abuse and then rejection.

I have worked with unmarried teen-age mothers over the years. Most of these girls I have worked with did not have a father present. The dads were absent because of desertion, divorce, or military duty, or they were emotionally gone because of alcohol or drug abuse. Tragedy of tragedies, these daughters of fatherless families all began fatherless families of their own.

WHEN CHILDREN DISAPPEAR

I close this chapter with the mention of yet one more of America's tragedies heavily energized by the missing dad syndrome—runaways. Over 150,000 children disappear each year in our nation. Most of them are runaways. Surprisingly, these children are not a result of financial poverty as much as they are of parental poverty displayed in the home.

"More than 80 percent of runaways are white, from middle and upper-middle-class families," writes Dotson Rader. "Without exception, those I met seemed starved for adult affection and regard, but fearful, filled with resentment against parents whom they believe never loved them. Oddly enough, they blame themselves and wonder what is so bad about them that made their parents love them so little.''[17]

Who could feel more unloved than the child whose father deserted him?

Father-absence in America is weakening the family structure with such drastic impact that some writers are gleefully awaiting its destruction with books like *Death of the Family*. In his famous book, *1984*, written in 1949, George Orwell predicted the breakup of the family and the dissolution of emotional family ties between men, women, and their children.

The problem of absent fathers is a matter of life and death to American families. The family is dangerously adrift in a violent sea of uncertainty. It has been severed from its anchor of genuine masculine leadership. Instead of helping the family regain its stability, the cowardly men of America are jumping ship at precisely the time in history when they should be leading their families to safe harbors.

Men have lost their grip on authentic manhood. It is vitally important that they regain it.

7

CONFESSIONS OF A FISH OUT
OF WATER

We know quite a bit about how boys develop and
grow; but at the same time, we have thought very little
about "masculinity," or about the kind of males we
want boys to be.

Patricia Sexton[1]

My wife is a schoolteacher. One day she was relating a deep
concern that she had for a troubled young boy who was having an extremely difficult time learning to spell. As I listened
to her, I was suddenly startled by an all-to-obvious fact I had
not realized before—almost *all* her problem students were
boys!

The public schools are inheriting critical problems among
male students because of father-absence in the home. The
question we must ask is, Does the public school system further promote the problem of the emasculation of the male, or
does it help him with his masculinity?

In Chapter 5, we traced historically how men have abdicated their responsibilities in the schools and churches of
America. In this chapter, we will consider the cost of that abdication that is being paid by young boys. Given the present
circumstances, I believe that every boy is being subjected to
powerful feminizing forces inherent in the current structure

of the elementary schools and Sunday schools of America. Permit me to be somewhat personal in the pages that follow as I make my point.

As much as we might want to resist it, the truth is that one of the most sacred cows of our culture, the American public school, has had tremendously negative effects on the masculinity of the males of our society. Only father-absence exerts a greater feminizing influence on our boys than do the schools of our land.

WHY IS JOHNNY NONACADEMIC?

Boys are entering American schools with startling disadvantages. It appears that from the very onset of their education, the deck is stacked against them. Patricia Sexton, professor of sociology and education at New York University, has directed research projects on poverty and the schools for the National Institute of Mental Health and the U.S. Office of Education. She reveals the following statistics:

- In mental institutions for children, boys outnumber girls three to one.
- More than two out of three students who fail one or more grades are boys.
- Pathological conditions, including learning and behavior disorders, are three to ten times as common among young males as among females of the same age.
- Among students who stutter, boys outnumber girls about four to one.
- About three out of four retarded readers are boys.

Sexton sums things up by saying, "Thus with respect to vision, hearing, speech, writing, manual and physical control— all the senses and physical capacities through which people *learn*—boys are disadvantaged."[2]

These facts have been borne out repeatedly in my wife's teaching experience. For the past ten years, she has been a special education resource teacher for three different elementary schools. This special education is a service of the public schools to children with learning handicaps. Without exception, the majority of her students have been boys. Recently, she has been working with twelve students who are so seriously disadvantaged that they have been removed from a regular classroom setting and put under her care on a full-time basis. Guess who the students are? All but one are boys.

Report cards of elementary school children show higher marks for girls than boys. Girls appear more often than boys on the honor roll, and they are not retained as often as boys. Girls also score higher on aptitude tests. There are more male than female underachievers.

There is a reason why boys do not do as well in the eyes of their teachers. When they enter school, they are ready to learn things that contribute to the formation of their masculinity, but they are not ready for the restrictions that come upon them from a feminine atmosphere. Therefore, compared to girls who easily conform to the feminine structure of the elementary school system, boys appear immature.

Because of this dilemma, every year the same question comes up from parents inquiring about the welfare of their five-year-old boy: "Should we wait one more year before we send our son to school? We don't want him lagging behind the others."

Even after their son has attended school, parents ask, "Do you think it will hurt our son to be retained one year? He seems to be a whole year behind the other students." These kinds of concerns expressed by parents almost always relate to boys.

Some experts say that boys are not mature enough to begin school until they are six and a half years old while girls seem to be ready for the classroom at age five years and nine months. I agree that many boys are not ready for school at the usual age of five. But this is not necessarily because they are immature. Could it not also be that teachers are not ready for normal five-year-old male behavior? *Momism* author Hans Sebald argues,

> All too often these boys' fundamental learning process is left exclusively to females—the mother, the Sunday school teacher, nursery and kindergarten personnel, and the elementary school teacher. Thus, boys are exposed to the continuous authority and teaching of agents whom they may not imitate, but whose guidance and information about what they should be they are expected to accept and practice.[3]

OUR SUNDAY WORST

My friends and I *hated* Sunday school. We thought it was worse than public school because we didn't have recess!

The members of my family never missed except in times of extreme illness. Although I'm thankful for my father's insistence on church attendance, I'm not thankful for the negative influence a feminized Sunday school had on me and my male friends. As I write, I can think of only a handful of friends out of a hundred or more children whose faith in Christ survived those early years.

Some of us boys sometimes tried to hurriedly force a recess between Sunday school and church. During one of these desperately sought-out breaks, a friend and I wandered into a neighbor's horse corral on the lot behind the church. Soon we were lost in the excitement of wrestling and tumbling in the mud in our Sunday suits.

A scream split the air and brought us back to reality. It was our Sunday school teacher. She was coming at us with nostrils flared and elbows extended like the wings of a large whooping crane. Her hands firmly gripped our rumpled jackets as she dragged us off to the pastor and our parents.

To this Sunday school teacher, we were bad boys, and she made no attempt to conceal that fact. Obviously, we were embarrassed by the public exposure. But inwardly, we were delighted to know that we weren't approved of by this pious, sentimental teacher who could not relate to young boys.

My friend Roger, who was a tough young man, and I entered the army together as soon as we graduated from high school. He and I had grown up in the same Sunday school, but he had become a church dropout. One evening we were lying on our bunks reminiscing about some of our childhood experiences when he said, "I really hated Sunday school except when your dad taught it." And he recalled a particular episode I'm sure none of the boys who were there have ever forgotten. In all candor, my father was not a gifted verbal communicator. Thus, he relied heavily on visual object lessons.

One Sunday morning, all of us fourth-grade boys were lined up on the backless wooden benches used in Sunday school. The story of David and Goliath was on the agenda. My father was attempting to describe Goliath, telling us how big and awesome the giant really was. We loved that story, but we'd heard it so often before that we weren't at peak attention.

All of a sudden, a roar that sounded like King Kong burst forth from a four-hundred-pound giant who landed in our midst! Wearing leather skins and wielding a huge club, he was a mountain of a man. We literally fell off our benches, and with horror-filled eyes, I watched Dad (who was small) grab a sling and slay the huge Nephilim. He fell with a crash at our feet.

Actually, the man whom Dad recruited to do the scene was a close friend and a real giant; he could pick up the rear end of a car or squeeze raw potatoes into juice with his bare hands. We *loved* it! It was visual, scary, and shocking, and our teacher was our hero of the day. Dad had no trouble applying the lesson to us that morning, convincing us that David was a real man—and a real man of God.

For a period of time, my friends and I could identify with being male and being Christian. But how rare are such experiences for boys in Sunday school!

It is common knowledge in every church circle I've ever been involved in that Sunday school teachers are overwhelmingly women. This circumstance is no accident. As we have seen documented, for a long time women have been given the task of nurturing the young people of the church and the school.

Evangelical curriculum writer and Wheaton College professor Paul Fromer warns, "Curriculum writers have got to do more to keep men in mind if they are going to hold them in the next decade."[4] In a *Christianity Today* article, "Is Sunday School Losing Its Punch?" Marlene Lefever, a David C. Cook Publishing executive, notes, "Men participate in Sunday School far less than women and perhaps our curriculum materials reinforce the idea that evangelicalism is a woman's religion."[5]

DEAR MISS BILLINGS

Although precise statistics demonstrating female preeminence in Sunday school are unavailable, that is not the case in the woman-dominated world of public elementary education. Remember, more than 83 percent of all teachers in public elementary schools are women![6] This works fine for girls who are ready to play school by participating in a feminine atmosphere. They sit quietly and listen to the teacher and take notes with their newly acquired skills in writing. Reading stories and gaining facts from books come easily for girls. They are usually eager to repeat the assignments that they have been asked to memorize.

Boys, on the other hand, are quickly bored with this seemingly passive style of schooling; they have little interest in sitting still and being quiet. Reading and memorizing do not fit into the real world of young males. No matter how many words pass through the air, staying seated in one place for long periods of time does not connect with the natural processes by which boys learn. And most boys intuitively know it.

Those first years in elementary school come at a time when a boy is developing inherent masculine tendencies. He is shaping his skills for courage and strength. Thus, he is constantly seeking action. While girls tend to want to think and feel, boys would rather see and do. They want to participate with vigorous verbal contact and aggressive physical action.

When class ends, the boys stampede the playground to accomplish some small acts of bravery. If a girl joins them, she is called a tomboy. Whether shooting at the air with gunbursts of imaginary bullets, hanging by the heels from playground bars, or simply shoving and pushing an opponent, boys will be (and need to be) boys. These very normal actions that boys display do not evoke the approval of a female-dominated system even on the school playground. What is natural to young males is often viewed as bad behavior. Therefore, many normal boys are labeled "bad boys" early in life when they are simply trying to discover their masculinity through innocent episodes of competitive game playing.

It was difficult enough to have a sister three years ahead of me in school, but the bigger problem was that she was an *A* student and an outstanding musician. Actually, things weren't too bad until I landed in Miss Billings's music class in the seventh grade. I had no interest in music since both my mother and my sister were pianists. I instinctively felt it would be disastrous for my painfully emerging manhood if I played the piano, too. But Miss Billings was not sympathetic. Within the first week in her class, she publicly mourned the fact that I was not a musician or a wonderful student like my sister.

That was fine by me. I didn't *want* to be like Joyce. She was

101

a girl, and I was a boy. If, in Miss Billings's class, being an achiever meant being like my sister, I was determined not to achieve, but to turn my creative resources to mischief. This woman, dedicated as she was, had done her part in teaching me the misconception that being masculine meant being "bad." No credit to me, she suffered greatly through prank after prank that I pulled on her for the rest of the semester.

Fortunately, I escaped the plight of many of my friends who ultimately gave up and joined the ever-growing army of high-school dropouts. They could no longer cope with the feminine system, and they simply left—blaming themselves as misfits within the walls of academia. Today, about three decades later, up to 30 percent of the students in some school districts of my home state of California drop out of high school. On a local level, my area's newspaper, the *Santa Cruz Sentinel*, reported that of the three hundred freshmen who entered Santa Cruz High School four years ago, only two hundred of them are still in school. Although a few moved out of the area, school district representatives insist that nearly all who left dropped out.[7] The statewide dropout rate in California has doubled since 1978.[8]

Other boys resolve the woman teacher–male student conflict by totally submitting to the system in order to obtain the academic awards bestowed upon achievers' heads. They become bookworms. Picture the young genius with his horn-rimmed glasses who seeks his teachers' approval to the point of alienating his male friends. For him, playground combat becomes a classroom mental game. He scratches and beats up other boys with his wit and caustic remarks.

Let me be quick to add that there are very masculine men who also excel academically. Not all honor students are wimps. Take Bill Bradley, a U.S. Senator who was not only a former Rhodes Scholar but also a professional basketball star as well. Or my good friend, Dr. Jack Sparks, a brilliant scholar and chancellor of a school of theology who was also a top-notch college jock. But men who excel academically and physically remain the exception, not the rule.

Patricia Sexton remarks:

> Besides noting the carnage left by the war between boy and school, I began this inquiry with the hunch, based on a life spent in classrooms, that boys who rise to the top in school often resemble girls in important ways. While they are a more diverse group, those boys who hide under the surface or sink to the bottom are less likely to be taken for girls. It is the baby fat that usually floats and the muscle that sinks. Scholastic honor and masculinity, in other words, too often seem incompatible.[9]

Unfortunately, it is usually this honor student who returns to the classroom to teach his feminized values to the young lads who enter his domain. For boys, the only thing worse than a woman teacher is a feminized man teacher who confuses and antagonizes them.

COACH SAM

In today's schools, one of the few reinforcers of masculinity is the male high-school coach. Sports provide a legal arena for boys to display a normal segment of their development.

Sam Della Maggiore was a well-known city councilman in San Jose who was also our high-school wrestling coach. We were aware that Sam didn't coach for the money; he did it because he loved sports and boys. That was enough to motivate us, but perhaps even more compelling was how we felt when we were around him—we felt like men.

This man chased away cowardice like vapor by his very presence. He was always encouraging us in our workouts by doing things like standing below us during the rope climbs and offering a friendly swat on our behinds with a paddle if we lingered within his swinging distance. He always took his team's side against any unjust referee or opponent. Coach

103

Sam insisted that each person do his best. For him, we couldn't do anything less. His masculine leadership resulted in his team's taking first place in the city's high-school wrestling league for *nineteen years straight*, the length of his career as a coach at San Jose High.

When Coach Sam retired, the team began to lose. What was his magic? I believe that in him young men recognized a true masculinity that combined strength, love, courage, and loyalty—the kind of example that young men need.

Athletics are the last frontier for boys to secure their identity as male. Now, even that is being tampered with. My son's elementary school soccer team was co-ed; all-girl teams are permissible, but all-boy teams are forbidden. A girl in a midwestern town has won a lawsuit to gain admittance to the local high-school football team. Similar developments are happening all over our nation. As we'll see in a later chapter, such feminist-inspired social changes are ultimately going to destroy true womanhood as well as true manhood.

America's schoolboys are troubled. From the very onset of their formal educational experience, they are subjected to a host of feminizing forces that create a sometimes unresolvable tug of war between being "good" and being "male." They are forced into making a choice they should never have to make.

All too often the end product of the American school system is a feminized young man who is unequipped to handle the responsibilities of mature manhood. It is time for men to move back into the leadership roles of both the churches and the public schools.

IT'S A CRIME TO BE MALE

We are going out of our way to grow irresponsible
males.

Phil Donahue[1]

The lack of adequate models of American masculinity, the
increasing numbers of passive and withdrawn fathers, and
the feminized approach to the major areas of education have
combined to produce modern males who are bastions of passivity and irresponsibility. This irresponsibility has under-
standably aroused an overwhelming barrage of hostile
accusations from the women and children of America. American masculinity has been on the "hot seat" for the last two
decades.

Observes sociologist-historian Peter Stearns:

Never before in the history of the species have groups of
women attacked men with more verbal violence than during
the past decade of the United States. Never before have the con-
ventions of gender differentiation been so thoroughly challenged. The initiative in the rhetoric of gender relationships is
clearly now in women's hands. Men can seem badly on the de-
fensive. Some feminists enjoy amazonian games, attacking
men as unnecessary and masculinity even as dangerous.[2]

Is Stearns exaggerating? Hardly. Famed anthropologist
Margaret Mead, whom Betty Friedan has called "the most

powerful influence on modern women," described a man's role as "uncertain, undefined, and perhaps unnecessary. By a great effort, man has hit upon a method of compensating himself for his basic inferiority."[3]

To these compliments about masculinity, the late feminist theorist Elizabeth Gould Davis added the following "insights":

> Maleness remains a recessive genetic trait like color-blindness and hemophilia, with which it is linked. The suspicion that maleness is abnormal and that the Y chromosome is an accidental mutation boding no good for the race is strongly supported by the recent discovery by geneticists that congenital killers and criminals are possessed of not one but *two* Y chromosomes, bearing a double dose, as it were, of genetically undesirable maleness.[4]

Did you get that? "Maleness is abnormal," "undesirable," "an accidental mutation" that results in "no good for the race." It is no longer *irresponsible* manhood that is under scrutiny. Maleness itself is now under attack.

The most tragic thing about this warped view of masculinity is that some men actually believe it. Every single day of the year, four Americans are so depressed, embarrassed, or confused about their gender that they submit themselves to sex-change operations. And despite the frustration and desperation of women, these sex-change operations are almost exclusively on men attempting to change their bodies into those of women. Being male is an increasingly undesirable state among growing numbers of American men. This male "inferiority complex" has got to go.

BAD BOYS

But getting rid of this bad feeling about the masculine gender is easier said than done. Its roots often run very deep. As we discussed a few pages earlier, numerous schoolboys find themselves caught in a desperate tension between being "good" and being "male." Patricia Sexton sums it up by saying that " 'Control' and 'discipline' in school usually mean, 'How do we tame the boys and get them to sit down and be quiet?' "[5]

The "bad boys" of today's elementary schools, more often than not, grow in patterns of irresponsible and antisocial behavior and become the juvenile delinquents of tomorrow. Fatherless boys, who are at odds with a feminized school system and have no adequate models of masculinity, are fanning the flames of teen-age violence and crime. Crime is so rapidly becoming a pastime of the young that University of Chicago criminologist Franklin E. Zimring concludes, "In a large measure, America's crime problem is its youth problem and vice versa."[6]

In 1982, more than eighty thousand juveniles were residing in juvenile custody facilities, not in their homes.[7] The year before that, over 51 percent of people arrested for what the FBI considers to be serious crimes were under the age of twenty.[8] *New York Times* writer William Shannon discloses, "Since 1963, crimes by children have been rising at a faster rate than the juvenile population . . . . The rate of armed robbery, rape, and murder by juveniles has doubled in a decade."[9]

Time magazine's Richard Stengel writes in an article on crime that young black men "seem to be murdering one another with a malign indifference, killing with the casual air of Bruce Lee dispatching men in a kung fu movie. For some, it seems as if murder has become a noxious fashion or wanton recreation."[10]

How does this escalation in juvenile crime translate into current statistics? The FBI estimates that in 1983, youths under the age of eighteen accounted for more than 218,000 burglaries, 81,000 drug abuse violations, 45,000 motor vehicle thefts, 43,000 aggravated assaults, and 10,000 arsons. In that same twelve-month period, over 5,600 women were raped by youths aged seventeen and under, and over 1,400 people were murdered by the children of America.[11]

A report entitled *Crime in America* states, "In 1981, a youngster between the ages of fourteen and seventeen stood about a one in thirty-three chance of being arrested. For all ages the chance was about one in 100."[12]

But who were these young perpetrators? You guessed it. They were overwhelmingly boys. The FBI reports that in 1983, there were 1,722,531 people under the age of eighteen arrested in this country. More than 78.7 percent of those arrested were boys. The arrest rate of boys is more than 365 percent higher than that for girls.[13]

What is causing young people, particularly boys, to commit so much of the serious crime in this country? The key common factor is the absence of a father. "Fatherless families . . . generate far more delinquency and personality disorders than do normal or motherless families," declares Daniel Amneus. "The delinquency ratio of children living with the mother only, compared to living with father only, is about three to one."[14] Society pays, for it provides the victims of the "bad boys" that have turned against it.

CRIME: A MALE AFFAIR

Do these fatherless delinquents learn their lesson from adolescent confrontations with the law? Usually not. They tend to behave even more irresponsibly. A *Washington Post* survey showed that almost two-thirds of adult prison inmates surveyed said they were involved in crime before their eighteenth birthday and that the "median age of an inmate's first incarceration was sixteen."[15]

Not only do criminals start young, but they are legion in number. The FBI reports that in 1983, there were over *two million* people arrested for murder, rape, robbery, assault, burglary, larceny, and arson.[16] No modern industrialized society kills, attacks, and steals with such frequency as America. Crime in the United States is growing faster than society is able to build prisons. Inability to provide facilities for the swelling criminal population haunts almost every state in the union.

Take trend-setting California, for example. In 1985, Governor George Deukmejian asked the legislature to set aside nearly $80 million for emergency prison construction. California's twelve state prisons are designed to hold 29,000 inmates. The current prison population of 49,000 shows how severe the overcrowding is. And the flow shows no signs of abating. New inmates are being added to the system at the rate of 166 per week.[17] At this pace, California's current prison population will double in less than six years! With good reason, people in the criminal justice system are running scared.

Who are these adult perpetrators? "FBI-compiled data from more than 15,000 jurisdictions around the country present a clear profile of the criminal, who is, by all means, a he. Males account for 81 percent of arrests, 90 percent of those for violent crimes, 79 percent of those for property-crime offenses."[18] Criminally irresponsible behavior in adults (as in juveniles) is an overwhelmingly male problem.

THE THRILL-SEEKERS

Yet criminality is just one irresponsible behavior exhibited by American men. Most men don't end up in jail, but that doesn't mean that they are necessarily responsible adults.

Take, for example, the single men of America. For the most part, they are the epitome of irresponsible self-indulgence. These spoiled, self-serving, self-seeking brats live in singles apartments and frequent singles bars; a primary goal is to try to find a mate for the night.

109

Single women are acutely aware of this situation. "The men I know are like children in a candy store," says Karen Swensen, twenty-eight, an interior designer. "There are so many women to choose from, they don't have to call on Monday for Saturday night. They have lists of names and numbers and, if one woman is busy, they go on to the next one. There is always someone who is available."[19]

Statistically, someone is always available because the odds are favorable to single men. "There are just under 30 million single women for 21.5 million single men" in America.[20] And single men seem to be making the most of this fact.

The greatest exploitation of the American woman comes not from the feminized husband, but from the feminized single male. This hedonist entrepreneur of pleasure takes advantage of a lonely woman who, in desperation, will cater to his every desire. As he does with countless disposable commodities, he throws away his woman as well. Always promising, never committing, he steals the vital, precious years of a young woman, and then he leaves her so that he can follow wherever his latest desire leads.

These men are not men at all. They prey on the vulnerability of single women whose fathers no longer protect them. And do we pay for their play! The government pays dearly for this recreational sex. In 1985, it cost the United States more than $16.5 billion to care for the single mothers and unwanted children left uncared for primarily by these "studs."

Most single men do not know that they are able to play their hedonistic games because some other male has failed to do his job. Real men, who protect the dignity of all women, are rare. They are hard to find, and it appears that the single women of America are desperate enough to pay to find them. I read that services devoted to helping women find men—clubs, study groups, classified ads, dating services, and the like—earned almost $40 billion in a recent year.

The single men of America need to leave the "candy store"

and mature. It's time for them to forget the "need for strokes" from surrogate mothers and begin to learn what it takes to be responsible men. Single men must stop acting like children with their overt displays of shameful self-indulgence and begin to treat the members of the opposite sex as persons of value. Older women should be treated as mothers and younger women as sisters. To ask this of a man calls for a responsible commitment, but only courageous men will make that decision and stick with it.

CRISIS IN BLACK AMERICA

Perhaps no other single segment of society suffers more from the national problem of irresponsible males than black families. That is not a racist statement. It is simply the honest, tragic truth that statistics tell.

In 1983, four out of ten black families in America had no father present, a ratio 300 percent greater than that of white families. More than half of all black children live with their mothers only.[21] And the percentage continues to escalate at alarming rates. It is too common to have to go back two or three generations in some black families to find a father who did not desert his wife and kids.

Missing men are a cancer that is destroying black families! For a variety of reasons, the problems of father-absence and male irresponsibility are at this time more pronounced in the black community than in the white population or in any other racial group. Through a history of slavery, segregation, exploitation, oppression, overwhelming prejudice, emasculation, and well-intentioned but degrading government assistance programs, black families have lost their leaders—the fathers.

This loss has overwhelming and fearful implications. The fatherless void among blacks has been a major factor in the current crime epidemic ravaging our nation. Remember, fa-

111

therless families produce more criminality. And since black families have a more frequent incidence of father-absence, they also have a more frequent incidence of criminal behavior. Blacks, who make up about 12 percent of the population, account for 46 percent of all male state and federal prison inmates. In 1981, a black man was over six times more likely to be incarcerated in a state or federal correctional facility than a white man.[22]

Even more startling and tragic are facts revealed in a *Time* magazine article that talks about

> a frighteningly familiar but largely unspoken national scourge: the epidemic of violence by young blacks against other young blacks. The leading cause of death among black males ages 15 to 24 in the U.S. is not heart disease, not cancer, not any natural cause. It is murder by other blacks. More than 1 out of every 3 blacks who die in that age group is the victim of a homicide. Across America, particularly among the underclass in the nation's urban ghettos, brother is killing brother in a kind of racial fratricide. More than 40% of all the nation's murder victims are black, and 94% of those who commit these murders are black. The 6,000 or so Americans who lost their lives because of black-on-black violence in 1981 alone rivals the number of black servicemen killed during the twelve years of the Vietnam conflict.[23]

The statistics add up to a horrifying equation. "In America today, a white female has 1 chance in 606 of becoming a murder victim. A white male has 1 chance in 186. A black female has 1 chance in 124. A black male has 1 chance in 29."[24]

John Dean, a black who serves on the Crime Compensation Board in Washington, D.C., discussed the gap between whites' and blacks' experience of crime in an ABC news interview:

> It's very difficult to live outside of a black community and perceive of the thinking and feeling that goes on inside. . . . It is

that all-pervasive fear because you never know, as I say, when you step out whether you're going to come back, and mostly when you're even in your house you don't have the sense of security that the majority population takes for granted.[25]

The fatherless black youth, in his flight from the feminizing forces of a matriarchal culture, has pursued the only option he sees available to him to gain masculinity. In his mind, being physically tough is masculine. And like Richard Pryor in the movie *Stir Crazy*, he nervously struts in front of his fellow prisoners with the self-assuring pronouncement of how "bad" he really is.

What can cure this desperate condition that plagues the lives of millions of Americans? Many worthy efforts are being made to alleviate this plight of American blacks. Neighborhood street patrols, community watches, and increased police protection have helped check crime. Alternative programs that create activities to replace territorial gangs are on the increase, easing some neighborhood tensions. Drives to improve education and to create employment are essential to reduce the crime rate in the black community.

Yet, none of these emphases have stemmed the tide because none of them touch on the real source of the problem. It seems that no one, for some hopeless or fatalistic reason, wants to touch on the raw nerve that needs to be healed—absent fathers.

Criminologist Marvin Wolfgang observes, "Poverty is not necessarily associated with crime because there are many more poor and law-abiding people."[26] If poverty were the main reason for crime, almost everyone in the Third World would be a criminal.

Daniel Amneus notes, "Investigators such as Loren Mosher of the NIMH (National Institute for Mental Health), Dr. Walter Mischel and others have found from cross-cultural studies they conducted that poverty is not as important a factor in juvenile delinquency as the absence of a competent and loving father."[27]

Crime is usually a problem for government to handle. But the Attorney General's Task Force on Violent Crime in 1981 questioned whether "a government, by the invention of new programs or the management of existing institutions, can by itself re-create those familial and neighborhood conditions, those social opportunities and those personal values that in all likelihood are the prerequisites for tranquil communities."[28]

The government can treat only the symptoms, and often it doesn't seem to do that very well. In fact, despite the good intent of all government programs, some of them have actually been more of a hindrance than a help. Some, such as Aid to Families with Dependent Children (AFDC), end up economically penalizing a man who wants to be married to the mother of his children. In his explosive book *Losing Ground*, social scientist Charles Murray conclusively demonstrates how governmental programs not only have failed to give adequate economic relief but have helped to further shatter already beleaguered poor black families.

According to Murray, a senior research fellow of the Manhattan Institute for Policy Research,

> the bottom line is this: Harold can get married and work forty hours a week in a hot, tiresome job; or he can live with Phyllis and their baby without getting married, not work, and have more disposable income. From an economic point of view, getting married is dumb. From a noneconomic point of view, it involves him in a legal relationship that has no payoff for him. If he thinks he may sometime tire of Phyllis and fatherhood, the 1970 rules thus provide a further incentive for keeping the relationship off the books.[29]

Such programs may provide some short-term relief, but they foster long-term devastation. They rob families, black and white alike, of the ingredient for success they presently lack—responsible men.

Please understand that I am *not* saying the impoverished economic conditions and the epidemic of crime that weigh so heavily and so disproportionately upon the shoulders of black Americans do not deserve increased and ongoing attention. What I *am* saying is that there is an even *greater* problem in black America than economic distress and lawlessness. It is a problem that lies at the root of so many other social dilemmas in the black community. It perpetuates poverty. It is a major contributing factor to crime. It is a problem that destroys the most essential of all social groupings—the family.

The greatest poverty in the black community is not measured in dollars and cents or in crime statistics. It is measured in the number of black households from which the father has disappeared. The greatest poverty of the black community is the same family bankruptcy now entangling all of America. The loss of fatherhood, coupled with other feminizing forces in our culture, is producing a young male who has never had the opportunity to discover his true masculinity because he's never had a father around as a model.

The hopeless, disillusioned young men of black America must be able to see and believe again that life is not hopeless, that they can make a difference. Faced by so many problems, they probably find it easy to believe that they really can't change much. That almost happened to Martin Luther King, Jr. In a meeting in Oslo, just after King was awarded the Nobel Peace Prize, his patriarchal father gave a "toast to God" for His blessings upon their family and for the honor that his son had brought to the Kings' name. Here is what happened next:

> They all applauded.
> Then King's mother rose.
> The room became silent. Only on rare occasions did his mother decide to speak.

"I want to tell you a story about myself that I am ashamed of," she said softly. "It's about the first time Martin spoke publicly. It was for a high school debate. Martin had worked very hard for it. Martin talked so well that everybody there knew he had won. But he was black and the other boy was white. So, of course, the other boy won." Her eyes became moist. "I'll never forget Martin's disappointment when he came home. And I said to him, 'Martin, you're not going to change the world. You're just a little Negro boy.'" She sighed wistfully. "I was trying to keep him from what I thought could be heartbreak. I was afraid for him. I almost did what millions of other black mothers do all the time—make our sons less." Smiling, she looked at her son with pride as well as tears in her eyes. "But one man *can* make a difference," she said. "And that's why we're here today."[30]

A CBS special, "The Vanishing Family—Crisis in Black America," poignantly examined the plight of the black family and rightly laid the majority of the blame for its disintegration squarely on the shoulders of irresponsible men. In a panel discussion of regional and national leaders of the black community, one participant notes something to the effect that "if Martin Luther King, Jr., were alive today he would not be talking about segregation; he'd be talking about saving the families of black America."

And what the black community so desperately needs is leaders who will call black men back to responsible manhood—leaders who will convince them that one man can make a difference in his home and in his community. Without that challenge and a proper response, I believe that the future is very bleak for the next generation of black children.

Our entire society has paid a heavy toll for the irresponsible men we produce. Juvenile delinquency, adult crime, self-indulgent single males, and vanishing families are just some of the consequences of absent and passive men who are unsure of their manhood. Only the rediscovery of a true masculinity will save us from the perils of our present state. But to recover traditional manhood, men will need a model to follow. So questions naturally arise: What does this model look like? How will men know the appropriate model? My next chapter will discuss some of the traits of a model for manhood.

A MODEL FOR MANHOOD

There is none like him on the earth, a blameless and
upright man.

Job 1:8

Throughout the summer of 1985, one of the top pop music
singles was Tina Turner's "We Don't Need Another Hero."
Seldom has a song missed the mark by so wide a margin. We
live in a time and culture desperate for heroes, people who
can be emulated and followed, people of courage. But what
are the guidelines for us to follow? Where do we turn for
help?

Women find an excellent set of standards to follow in
"their" famous Bible chapter, Proverbs 31. How many sermons or challenges have you heard in your lifetime on the
Proverbs 31 woman or the Proverbs 31 wife? Let me suggest
that there is a chapter in the Bible, also from the Old Testament, for men as the model for masculinity. Let's hear it for
the Job 29 man! Here men can find God's idea of what real
manhood is.

NINE TRAITS OF
BIBLICAL MASCULINITY

Job, best known as a survivor of great suffering, also stands
as an incomparable image of manhood. In him are the essential attributes for men to rediscover if they are to free themselves from the shackles of a feminized culture.

118

Job lived near the dawn of civilized humanity. The book named after him, according to many Christian and Hebrew scholars, is the oldest in the entire Bible. He is remembered—indeed venerated—in sacred and secular circles alike as a man of enormous staying power; in fact, "the patience of Job" is a phrase that has become a part of our everyday language.

The crucially important characteristics revealed about Job in chapter 29 of the book bearing his name make a good definition of what real masculinity is all about. Here is that chapter:

> Job further continued his discourse, and said:
> "Oh, that I were as in months past,
> As in the days when God watched over me;
> When His lamp shone upon my head,
> And when by His light I walked through darkness;
> Just as I was in the days of my prime,
> When the friendly counsel of God was over my tent;
> When the Almighty was yet with me,
> When my children were around me;
> When my steps were bathed with cream,
> And the rock poured out rivers of oil for me!
>
> "When I went out to the gate by the city,
> When I took my seat in the open square,
> The young men saw me and hid,
> And the aged arose and stood;
> The princes refrained from talking,
> And put their hand on their mouth;
> The voice of nobles was hushed,
> And their tongue stuck to the roof of their mouth.
> When the ear heard, then it blessed me,
> And when the eye saw, then it approved me;
> Because I delivered the poor who cried out,
> And the fatherless and he who had no helper.
> The blessing of a perishing man came upon me,
> And I caused the widow's heart to sing for joy.
> I put on righteousness, and it clothed me;
> My justice was like a robe and a turban.

I was eyes to the blind,
And I was feet to the lame.
I was a father to the poor,
And I searched out the case that I did not know.
I broke the fangs of the wicked,
And plucked the victim from his teeth.

"Then I said, 'I shall die in my nest,
And multiply my days as the sand.
My root is spread out to the waters,
And the dew lies all night on my branch.
My glory is fresh within me,
And my bow is renewed in my hand.'

"Men listened to me and waited,
And kept silence for my counsel.
After my words they did not speak again,
And my speech settled on them as dew.
They waited for me as for the rain,
And they opened their mouth wide as for the spring rain.
If I mocked at them, they did not believe it,
And the light of my countenance they did not cast down.
I chose the way for them, and sat as chief;
So I dwelt as a king in the army,
As one who comforts mourners."

I have identified nine traits exhibited by Job in this chapter. Let's look at each one individually and see how it fits into the model for manhood.

1. A Sense of Continuity with the Past

Job was a man who had a sense of continuity with the past. He valued the past, but not as one who pines for "the good old days" in order to keep from dealing with present realities. Rather, he valued the past because of the truth it taught him about God, about people, and about himself. It helped him put current events in a proper perspective. Through remembering how God had dealt with him in the past, Job was able to endure his present suffering.

What a contrast to modern American males. They, too, are

undergoing a certain amount of present suffering. But unlike Job, they act as if they had no past from which to learn. In fact, they seem to exercise a subtle contempt for the past. They may be awed by time-enduring triumphs of art, architecture, and craftsmanship of ancient times, but they brush off as absurd the thought that yesterday's ideas about men, their families, or their God could be of any possible help to enlightened moderns.

Men may talk about the wisdom of Solomon, but how many of them actually look to his proverbs for instruction in raising their children? Aren't they more likely to follow the advice of the latest pop psychologist? And what of their own lifestyles and value systems? It seems that talk-show hosts and Madison Avenue advertising agencies, not Solomon or the Bible, influence the men of modern America.

Giant technological and scientific strides in the last century have lulled Americans into making the erroneous assumption that we must have also made great improvements in human relationships. Therefore, we reason, we need not look to the past for instruction on how to raise a family or how to be a man any more than we would for advice on the fastest way to move the U.S. mail. We tend to believe that newer must be better. But even a cursory glance at the headlines of any major newspaper on any day will clearly show that in the realm of human relationships we are doing no better, in fact are probably doing worse, than those who went before us.

Haven't you ever wondered why marriages used to work, why family members got along reasonably well, why there wasn't a perpetual and almost frantic search for "alternative lifestyles"? It's hard to find satisfactory answers to these questions when words such as *tradition* and *godliness* have been contemptuously relegated to the realm of the irrelevant.

But tradition really means nothing more than, as G. K. Chesterton said, giving our ancestors a vote. Who knows? We might even learn a few things if we ask our aged relatives what things worked well for them instead of shunting them off to a retirement village or an old-age home.

Even the church did better when she maintained a link with the entirety of past generations. Could it be that Paul knew what he was talking about when he told the Christians at Thessalonica, "Stand fast and hold [to] the traditions which you were taught"?[1]

Men will never fully recapture their missing manhood until they repent of modern arrogance and humbly look at the history of American masculinity to see what truths it has to pass on to them. Each man's personal past and the histories of others are wonderful instructors. Men isolate themselves from the past at great peril. They are not islands. All of male history is their history.

2. A Man Remains Close to His Children

One of the first things mentioned about Job was that he was a father. But something about Job's fathering stands in stark contrast to the way so many modern American men operate today.

In the midst of his suffering and exile, Job said he missed having his children around him. He obviously did not view children as an intrusion into the pursuit of his personal pleasure. On the contrary, they were a prime source of his pleasure.

Job's concern for his children went beyond seeing that they had a roof over their heads and food in their stomachs. In his mind, fathers were obliged to care for the spiritual needs of their offspring as well. Job did not leave the religious state of the children up to Mrs. Job or the "Sabbath school" teacher. He took charge of their spiritual development. He was devoted to their well-being. Look at the evidence.

From an earlier passage in the book of Job, we learn that he would get out of bed early in the morning to offer sacrifices in behalf of his children:

> He would rise early in the morning and offer burnt offerings according to the number of them all. For Job said, "It may be that my sons have sinned and cursed God in their hearts."[2]

So Job prayed and meditated before the Lord on their behalf.

Job had ten children, by the way. Not a small family by any means. Yet, he took pains to be intimately involved in securing the physical and spiritual care of each of his seven sons and three daughters. You'd think that with that many children he would be all "fathered" out. But he wasn't. His children were a priority with him.

3. A Father to the Fatherless

Job was also actively involved in the care and guidance of children beyond the walls of his own home. He helped the poor and the fatherless.

I have fond childhood memories about the way my father cared for the poor. I can remember my sister and I riding in the back seat of Dad's 1940 Pontiac on Sunday afternoons as we took groceries to some "poor people."

One hot summer day as we were going to make yet another delivery of food, my mother commented that we really didn't have very much food for ourselves. Dad replied, "We have more than these people do." That was the end of the conversation.

How many of the single mothers of America could use the help of a Job today? And how many of the millions of fatherless children under the age of eighteen could be saved from great harm if there were more men like Job around?

May I say a careful word here? Boys don't need "big brothers" as much as they need fathers. If a man joins one of the helper agencies to assist young men without fathers, he

123

should be a father to them, not just a bigger kid on the block. He should show them the fullness of fatherhood.

Biology is not what makes one truly paternal. As Clayton Barbeau writes, "The conscious sense of responsibility for the physical and spiritual well-being of others is the mark of a true father."[3]

4. An Enforcer of Justice

Part of the incredible power that draws millions of men and boys to embrace the twentieth-century celluloid superhero of today as portrayed by Stallone, Eastwood, Schwarzenegger, or Norris is the thirst for justice. Wanting to see offenders punished and the enemy destroyed is a basic orientation put into men by God. To be a true man is to want this justice.

Like a suit of clothes, Job covered himself with this kind of justice and took it with him in every encounter of life. "My justice was like a robe and a turban," he said.

Always wanting to be fair, never making a judgment without listening to both sides, knowing that condemnation without investigation is foolish, Job said, "I searched out the case that I did not know." But when he found injustice—watch out! If he saw evil ones preying upon the innocent, he took aggressive action and "broke the fangs of the wicked, / And plucked the victim from his teeth."

"Cruel, harsh words!" comes the cry from our nice-guy society. "This Job person is into uncivilized talk. Such barbaric and aggressive orientation within men must go. It does not belong in a refined twentieth-century America."

Hostile charges against men's natural inclination to aggressively seek justice involve a play on feminized emotions. They are a sneaky, disarming attempt to strip males of their manhood—to make them feel guilty over something innately masculine. Real men get angry over injustice. Therefore, it is essential that today's men resist guilt for thinking, acting, and feeling the way real men think, act, and feel.

124

I'm not talking about having a vengeful spirit. Revenge is usually occupied with getting even for some personal grievance. Job's desire to see injustice punished did not come forth for his own sake but for the sake of others. In all the things that God allowed to come Job's way, several were the result of injustice. Thieves stole his oxen, donkeys, and camels. But there is no record of his organizing a posse to recover his property. He had great patience regarding wrongs he personally suffered. But you had better not mess with the widows and orphans!

Most women would probably not have acted like Job. They would not "feel right" about it. And naturally so. They would have more likely prayed for mercy because that is a basic orientation given to woman from God. Please understand that I am not saying that women have no desire for justice or that men lack compassion. I'll show in a moment that Job was also a man of mercy. I'm speaking in generalities. But when speaking about American men as a whole one must speak of the norm and not the exception. And usually men's desire for justice is stronger than their propensity to give mercy, and the opposite is true of women. That's why when little Johnny comes home bruised and bloody from an encounter with the neighborhood bully it is usually Mom who seeks to comfort Johnny while Dad is already thinking of how to see that the bully gets dealt with. When woman's feelings for mercy become the rule of practice over man's innate sense for justice, society will lose its sharp cutting edge for what is right and wrong.

Let me ask you this question: Would a woman have cleansed the temple of God with a whip and turned over the tables of the moneychangers? Today, the answer would probably be yes. But only because the men of today would be too "nice" to kick corruption in the seat of the pants. The fact is, we need both justice and mercy.

Like Job, men were created to demand justice in all things.

In the Scriptures, we are told to be angry and sin not[4]—that is, to be angry without passion at the things that are destroying our faith, our homes, and our children. The fact that men were created to desire and aggressively seek justice, to want to see offenders punished and the enemy destroyed, is an essential part of the manly courage needed to take action in the world in which we live.

5. Godly Mercy

What made Job stand for justice at all costs? Unlike many other men of material wealth in history, Job was also a man of *mercy*. His wealth did not stop his ears to the cries of people asking for help or blind his eyes to their plight. Job was out there making it happen; he was a rescue mission on two feet.

Today's men talk about helping the poor. But from my own observation, the ones who strike the loudest cymbals to harangue the rich into giving to the poor usually never leave their academic environments to do the work themselves. Others, because of their laziness, have never acquired enough to have something to give anyway. Both talk the talk but don't bring mercy into reality by offering a flesh-and-blood hand to a single impoverished soul who bears a personal name.

Job was different. He actively pursued the needy. Like the good Samaritan, he went out of his way to provide a strong, merciful hand. And all those who witnessed the unselfish demonstrations of mercy were amazed:

> "When the eye saw, then it approved me;
> Because I delivered the poor who cried out,
> And the fatherless and he who had no helper."

Job was the kind of man people wanted near them at the most critical time of their lives—the moment of impending death. Remember his words: "The blessing of a perishing man came upon me."

The twentieth-century American wife would be happy to have a contemporary Job as her husband, and the husbandless mother would be pleased to benefit from his generosity. Job said, "I caused the widow's heart to sing for joy." Mercy made wealthy Job both real and tangible to his community. It made him blameless. He was honored and respected. Nevertheless, mercy did not reign at the expense of justice. Job was merciful, and he was also just; mercy and justice meet together in a real man.

6. A Receiver of Respect

Unlike humorist Rodney Dangerfield, Job was a man who got all the respect he could handle. His presence alone altered the behavior of those around him. No one could ignore him. His deeds were so awesome and his actions so courageous that other men met him with honor fit for a king.

This man of God's own choosing did not, by the way, *demand* respect. He got it the old-fashioned way—he earned it! Job wasn't born with fully developed spiritual gifts and manly characteristics. He labored hard to develop them as any righteous man would do. I believe Job diligently pursued those virtues and characteristics that reflected the privilege that all men share in being made in the image and likeness of God. Job, through practice, had his senses trained to discern good and evil.

No one could be neutral in Job's sight. Nobody abstained from voting when he was around. Foolishness fled from his sight. Job tells us as much:

> "When I went out to the gate by the city,
> When I took my seat in the open square,
> The young men saw me and hid."

Those who desired wisdom and knowledge received this man. They welcomed him like a triumphant hero coming home from the conquest:

127

"The aged arose and stood;
The princes refrained from talking,
And put their hand on their mouth;
The voice of nobles was hushed,
And their tongue stuck to the roof of their mouth.
When the ear heard, then it blessed me,
And when the eye saw, then it approved me."

Some of the families in our church received eleven Japanese girls into their homes as exchange students. At the end of the four-week stay, one man pressed the girls with a specific question: "What was the most disturbing thing to you about us Americans?"

Their reply? "Disrespect for elders."

I agree with them. The next question is, How do we regain it?

If a man does not *pursue* wisdom, mercy, and justice, what is there to respect? Wives are told in the Holy Scriptures to respect their husbands. But let's be honest. Who has killed their respect? Men, that's who. Men today are making it almost impossible for women to respect them. I know of large numbers of Christian women who respect and honor their husbands out of obedience to the Lord, not because of their husbands' persistent, merciful, no-nonsense holiness. Job gained the respect of others because of his true manliness, and he also had the respect of God Himself!

7. A Life of Permanence

The stability of Job's lifestyle stands in vivid contrast to the anxious mobility that permeates our society where almost 25 percent of the population moves each year. The temporariness of American neighborhoods prevents us from building a sense of community and keeps us from experiencing the security and identity that such stability can bring. In the words of Vance Packard, we have indeed become "a nation of strangers."

Job desired the order and peace that permanence brings to families. He had no greener pastures to move to. He intended to "die in [his] nest." He set down roots that "spread out to the waters." He wanted to grow old in the place of his abode where he would "multiply [his] days as the sand."

Some people have mistakenly identified this desire to stay put as unmasculine. They think "real men" are continually riding off into the sunset like the Western movie hero. But it takes a man who is much more a man to put down roots. One of the most masculine men I know has written:

> I recall when I was growing up back in a small Texas town, there were events which helped bring me identity. I knew everyone within a two-block radius. My friends were my neighbors. The people across the back alley were the Roberts—Mr. and Mrs. E. T. Roberts. They had five sons and one daughter: Everett, Matt, Wallace, Ronny, Donny, and Geneva. I *knew* these people; they were my close friends. I did not have to drive 40 miles to see my friends. I could walk out the back door and there they were.
>
> Across the street were the Hawkins, and the Rushes lived on the other side. Across the way were the MacDonalds, the Kendalls, the Venables. Because I knew all these folks I did not have any critical loss of identity when growing up. I had identity in terms of the community in which I lived. And that was very important for me, for my own security. It created in me a very "belonging" experience in my upbringing.[5]

Real men are secure and have a strong sense of personal worth. It's extremely difficult for people to build this healthy identity when they are always on the move. An unending string of moves is one of the chief causes of the high rate of marital and family problems in military families.

Some of the most problem-ridden families I work with are those who never stay put. They move on before they are able to become a stable part of the community, on to a new town, a new neighborhood, a new church. Always changing schools and friends, their children become sadly insecure. These people are always planning their next move. With one eye on you and one eye on the front door, they become the double-minded people the Bible describes, unstable in all their ways (see Jas. 1:8).

I must admit that I was one of those men who kept moving from place to place. Like many others, I wanted my life to be totally committed to the Christian cause. I willingly and obediently responded to the constant pulpit challenge to "go." I was a "go-go Christian," and the sad thing is that nobody told me to "stop" for the next ten years. By then, I had moved my family six times. Fortunately, in the early seventies, with the help of some other men in the ministry, I came to the understanding of how important it is for a man to put down roots. I've never moved since then. And is my family glad!

Men who have moved too many times in pursuit of greener pastures should consider saying no to the next job promotion if it means uprooting the family one more time. Maybe moving would be more lucrative, but staying put would be the best for the family. Men were created to choose what is right. Since the days of Abraham, it has, on occasion, been the will of God for men to relocate their families. However, before we make such a move we had better be *certain* that moving is God's will rather than some impulsive vision rooted in greed or irresponsibility.

Men have foolishly sacrificed part of their personal peace and identity on the altar of mobility, and in doing so, they seem to have forgotten something Job knew very well. Real men bring order, peace, and identity to their families by not allowing them to be constantly uprooted.

8. A Well of Wisdom

The great Solomon did not have the wisdom market completely cornered. Job had a lion's share of it, also. He was everything E. F. Hutton ever dreamed of being. When he spoke, everybody listened:

> "Men listened to me and waited,
> And kept silence for my counsel.
> After my words they did not speak again."

He didn't just flap his lips. Job had true wisdom. Not political rhetoric born of personal ambition and manipulation. Not arrogant and scholastic verbiage flowing from an ivory tower. Not contentless, emotional, and persuasive speech that faded away when the aroused feelings died. Truth, made clear by the insight of true wisdom, is born of God, and Job had that wisdom. He feared God, and all men who fear God have at least attained the beginning of wisdom.

When I worked in San Bernardino, California, my friend Bob Cording and I used to visit an elderly black man whose name was Mr. Parker. He owned a junkyard. In the midst of all the clutter of his business stood a little shack that always gave the sense of a place of peace. A picture of Christ met our eyes as we entered the door. An old, worn, well-read Bible with pages soiled by working hands lay on a shelf.

Mr. Parker had an unusually distinguished dark face that was crowned with a head of white hair. Somehow, his faded flannel shirt and baggy pants did not seem right on him. To us, he should have been dressed like a monarch or a statesman.

Bob and I usually called on people to tell them about Christ. But when we visited Mr. Parker, we went to listen. Even though he was the son of slaves and had never been to school, our friend was an extremely wise man—"street smart," as we say today. He had used his ninety years on this planet to gain truth and knowledge from his observations of man and God. His exhortations and advice dropped on our ears like sounds from another world, yet they were simple enough for young men like us to understand. We always left

131

inspired, saying to ourselves and to each other, "Why hadn't we ever thought of that?"

So it was with Job. He said,

> "My speech settled on them as dew.
> They waited for me as for the rain,
> And they opened their mouth wide as for the spring rain."

When was the last time modern men were praised for being laden with godly wisdom? The need for wisdom is not even a topic for talk anymore. More than growth stocks or grain futures, let men set their hearts on gaining wisdom as the true treasure. Whoever loves wisdom makes those around him rejoice. Wisdom gives life. Wisdom gives strength. And wisdom gives a good defense because it comes from God. But with the loss of manhood, men have lost the desire for this great pearl. Job shows us that real men seek wisdom, and men today won't recover their lost masculinity without it.

9. A Pursuer of God

Beyond all his other character traits, Job was, first and foremost, a pursuer of God. Pursuit of God is a mark of a real man. That can sound foreign to us who live in a culture where religion has, for years, been the domain of women. The last few generations of American males have often seen women as the primary pursuers of God.

A friend told me that most of his childhood years were spent under the impression that Christianity was for women and their children. "What else could I think?" he said. "For years Dad dropped my mom, me, my brother, and my sister off at church every Sunday morning while he went back home and watched the football game. A lot of my friends had the same taxi service at their house. I learned at an early age that being a man and serving God somehow didn't go together."

But Job never saw such a dichotomy between manliness and piety. In fact, for him, a relationship with God the Father was the foundation of all his other manly virtues. How else can a man have absolutes by which his masculinity is defined?

It was because of God's mercy that Job was merciful to the needy. It was because God is just that Job sought justice for the oppressed. It was because God hates evil that Job broke the fangs of the wicked. His life, in all its masculine expression, was built around his worship of God. His pursuit of God molded him into the kind of man he was. That is why God approved Job as a *model for true mankind*. That is why God referred to Job as "a blameless and upright man, one who fears God and shuns evil."[6]

How did those around him view this man who centered his life on God? As an obnoxious, holier-than-thou Bible thumper? As a heartless legalist or a pious prude? Hardly.

The Father Himself calls men to be holy as He is holy. Men today seem to feel either that they are hopelessly created evil and weak and not able to gain righteousness or that holiness is a liability to manhood.

Most important of all, Job had the courage to keep his commitment to the Lord. Many people have suffered, but the whole world knows no one has suffered like Job. Newspaper headlines compared the devastation of the earthquakes in Mexico to the "trials of Job." Such is his fame. Job, caught between two kingdoms in a test of courage and loyalty, suffered the loss of everything—his children, servants, livestock, and land. Reduced to ashes, he cried out,

> "Naked I came from my mother's womb,
> And naked shall I return there.
> The LORD gave, and the LORD has taken away.
> Blessed be the name of the LORD."[7]

What a put-down of the modern American man, who so easily abandons his own home and demolishes his children for self-gratification or because he can't cope with the daily pressures of leading and guiding his family into the riches of an ordered, stable life.

Job was a real hero and a model for all men to follow and imitate. Imagine! God said he was blameless. That's enough for me to put him on my list of real men. May such men walk the streets of our world once again!

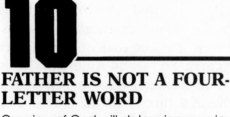

FATHER IS NOT A FOUR-LETTER WORD

Our view of God will determine our view of man.
J. Richard Ballew[1]

The American family is vanishing before our very eyes. The young people of some segments of society are already self-destructing. Feature articles in magazines and newspapers throughout the land are shouting out the startling statistics of the family dilemma primarily caused by irresponsible men. Ivory-towered professors and political opportunists are seen meeting together on national television bemoaning the problem, frantically suggesting a return to a sense of moral reality—but no one is saying how!!

Most everyone agrees we desperately need a return to morality. But the question is, Who in pluralistic America is going to define moral acts? The revolutions of the late sixties and early seventies challenged the meaning of and reasons for traditional absolutes. Nobody could recall where moral values came from. No longer could we say that being moral is right—just "because"! No longer could men be masculine just because they were born men. No longer could people get married and stay married just because that's the right thing to do. No longer was having children an unchallenged event.

135

Everything was challenged. No traditional stone was left unturned. And the question most frequently asked was, WHY? Why be moral? Why be men? Why be married? Why raise children?

American leaders are still faced with those same haunting questions. Why should the men of America assume the moral responsibility for their homes and imprint the absolutes of right and wrong on their children once again? It takes a courageous and godly man to answer that question, because it just might cost him dearly. So far, no American leader who has the ear of this nation's citizens has rallied the war-torn remnants of the traditional family to the sound of a clear trumpet call—a mighty trumpet blast so loud it will drown out the distracting yelps of the special interest groups such as the gays and the radical feminists who smartly rally into voting blocs and effectively prevent American leaders from reaching any consensus about the plight of the irresponsible American male.

A moral and a spiritual war is raging in our land that can be won only by men who know who they are and who are willing to confront the enemies of authentic manhood. A new era of righteous and manly men must, as the legendary phoenix, rise from the ashes.

A MAN AS FATHER

It has been my thesis that the present unraveling of American society exists in large part because of our cultural disdain for fatherhood. Responsibilities of fatherhood are being ducked. Fatherhood has been gutted of honor and respect until the most common portrayal of an American father is the spineless, bumbling idiot of television's situation comedies. At a time when responsible fathers are America's greatest need, men are abandoning family leadership and giving in to an adolescent attraction to hedonistic pleasure.

But such a course is suicidal for America. Throughout the history of mankind, civilization has been held together by fatherhood. Fatherhood is so essential to the proper ordering and smooth functioning of life that no society can long endure without it.

Amazingly, the problem of the irresponsible father is singled out in the very last verses of the Old Testament. The ancient prophet Malachi, speaking of John the Baptist and of his calling the nations to repentance, seems to also explain why our land is plagued with so many ills. The prophet, speaking for God, says,

> "Behold, I will send you Elijah the prophet
> Before the coming of the great and dreadful day of the LORD.
> And he will turn
> The hearts of the fathers to the children,
> And the hearts of the children to their fathers,
> *Lest I come and strike the earth with a curse*".[2]

Experts agree that the major problems troubling America, such as juvenile delinquency, violent crime, suicide, and illegitimate birth, stem from fathers who have turned their hearts from their children. What will it take for American manhood to rise from the rubble of a disintegrating society? American masculinity will awaken from its present pathetic state only when the men of this country are willing to be fathers.

That's right. I said fathers. Fatherhood and true manhood are inseparable.

SPIRITUAL FATHERS

All men are called to be spiritual fathers, even single males and childless husbands. Men who are not biological fathers are still called upon to devote time, effort, and energy to the guidance and care of the young people around them, comforting, counseling, and instructing those who have no dads.

137

There is a desperate need for the single men and childless husbands of our nation to imitate God, the Father of us all, who is described as a "father of the fatherless."[3]

At this point a Christian might well ask, "Aren't you linking masculinity and fatherhood much too closely? Isn't Jesus Christ our highest standard for what it means to be manly? Yet He Himself is not a father."

Jesus Christ *is* a father. As Adam was the father of a fallen race, so Jesus Christ is the father of the new race. In fact, Isaiah's accurate prophecy concerning the Incarnation explains why one of the titles to be given to the Son of God would be "Everlasting Father."[4]

What's going on here? As to the Trinity, don't we keep the Father and the Son distinct? Absolutely! Jesus is not a father in relation to the Trinity, but He is in relation to His church. When Isaiah called Jesus Christ the Everlasting Father, he was speaking of the age to come when He would be a father of the new covenant. The first Adam was the father of the human race while Christ, the Second Adam, is the father of the new race that is born in Him. Thus, the Son of God the Father has Himself the attributes of fatherhood. Jesus' words are true when He says, "He who has seen Me has seen the Father."[5] In revealing the Father, He as father of the faithful is the perfect expression of fatherhood. He is the progenitor of the new humanity! Jesus Christ's role as both father *and husband* constitutes the basis for an official male priesthood in the historic church. A subcommittee of the Ecumenical Task Force of the Orthodox Church in America writes in its book, *Women and Men in the Church,*

> Bishops and priests in the Church are sacramentally ordained to actualize the presence and power of Jesus Himself in the Church, Christ's own personal and individual presence and activity as the good pastor, the great high priest, the head of the body, the husband of the churchly spouse, the bridegroom of his pure bride. In order for the bishop and priest to complete

his sacramental task for the sake of the whole Church, therefore, he must be one who can image, symbolize, and mystically actualize the Lord's presence as husband and father of the flock. It is impossible for a woman to exercise this ministry and to fulfill this task.[6]

And not only that, Christ in His incarnation did in fact exalt His earthly mother Mary, the new Eve, to be the first of the redeemed in the church and also the human mother of the church. All men—married or single—can follow Christ in fatherhood, being spiritual fathers of those they bid to follow Him. If single men and childless husbands of this country see that God's call to fatherhood extends to them as well as to biological fathers, perhaps some of the millions of children who have no father present will have a chance of making it.

Real men do not just make babies. Real men take responsibility for the physical and spiritual care of children they beget and for those begotten and deserted by others. Responsibility lies at the heart of fatherhood as it was intended to be.

WHAT'S IN A WORD?

Where did the role of fatherhood come from? The essence of fatherhood is best understood in one word that Americans, even Christian Americans, have totally lost the meaning of, a word against which all the enemies of God have warred in an attempt to secure its annihilation. A word that has been abused, trampled on, ignored, or vehemently spit upon and mocked by raging hyperfeminists and discarded by irresponsible, self-centered, hedonistic males. A word so powerfully significant and loaded that the feminized, peace-at-any-price boys religiously relegate it to ancient days of antiquity. A word that has become unmentionable among its owners and exiled to the company of obscene four-letter words in the minds of most male and female Americans.

But whether we use this word or not, without its recovery, without its function being made known and its reality working in society, there is absolutely no clear, positive way to redeem the male identity. This word can never be neutral. It was worn by the men of old, from Abraham to David, and it needs to belong to American men today.

What is this awesome word that must be understood? This role that must be reclaimed? The word is *patriarchy*. It is awesome because it is in the meaning of this word that fatherhood exists and the foundation of the male identity is supplied.

The biblical term *patriarchy* is derived from two words in the Greek language—*patria* (taken from the word *pater*, "father"), which means "family"; and *arche*, which means "beginning," "first in origin," and "to rule." A patriarch is a family ruler. He is the man in charge. But to understand his role and function—and to help defuse the emotions of those who have been hurt or embittered by bad fathers—let us go all the way back to the foundation of all patriarchy: God the Father.

THE FORGOTTEN FATHER

I don't know about you, but I grew up with little understanding of God the Father. In fact, the church my parents attended had evolved out of the revival fires of the Second Great Awakening. In the church's desire for total independence and for the vision of restoration of the "New Testament church," it rejected all the ancient creeds held by serious Christians throughout the centuries.

Many new creeds took their place, however, such as "We speak when the Bible speaks and we are silent where the Bible is silent" or "We have no creed but Christ." We dutifully learned these creeds as small children.

But none of them mentioned God the Father. I heard the

140

Father referred to in the Scriptures, but He had no real place in my mind and heart. Jesus Christ was, in all practicality, the only person of the Trinity who counted. Later, in my involvement with mainline evangelical groups, I found that the Holy Spirit was emphasized along with Christ as a divine person I needed to know. All this was good and true as far as it went, but it was not enough to give me a proper view of the Holy Trinity—or of myself. God the Father was still a vague, dim figure who had somehow been relegated to Old Testament history. He seemingly had no involvement in His creation, much less as the One to be the ultimate model for human fathers.

Our favorite evangelistic Scripture was, "I am the way, the truth, and the life." But for some reason, we left off the other half of that passage, "No one comes to the Father except through Me."[7] The emphasis was on Christ as "the way," not on the supreme purpose of Christ's mission to bring us to the Father.

Men must turn back to knowing God as Father, and the Father they must return to is no sweet, feminized, pie-in-the-sky, absentee deity. He is the Patriarch of patriarchs. He is the ultimate reason that men should behave responsibly. There is no hope for the feminized fathers of America unless they return from the exile of self-serving and unaccountable behavior and offer their souls to the mercy of the Father who created them.

This is what happened to the apostle Paul at his conversion; this is how he became the spiritual father we acknowledge him to be. He said that he bowed his "knees to the Father of our Lord Jesus Christ, from whom [all fatherhood] in heaven and earth is named."[8] And in so doing, he related all fatherhood to His fatherhood.

Therefore, before men can discuss and, in humility, practice true patriarchy, they must turn to the God who is the Patriarch of all, the Father from whom all fatherhood is derived. Along with the apostle Paul, fathers must bow their knees to

141

that Father, confessing and embracing what is true about Him before they can discover what is true about themselves. Their view of the fatherhood of God will determine their view of the fatherhood of man.

God the Father set the criteria that men were created to fulfill. The eternal plan for man is not up for grabs or for change by twentieth-century "new age" concepts or by the enlightened antifamily spirit of self-indulgence that leads the spirit of this age. After all, the Father is God. He is in charge. He is Patriarch.

Thomas Howard writes in his book, *Splendor in the Ordinary*, that God

> did not sit down at a round table with the patriarchs and say, "Here, let me sketch out the rationale for my plan for you and get some feedback from you on it." The prophets did not say, "Let's have some input from everyone and see what the consensus is." The apostles did not say, "Give us your insights, and we'll try to paste together some sort of evangel." Sooner or later there is a *dictum* in this universe, and we men are indebted, nay we owe our life and salvation, to the fact that somebody said to us "Thus saith the Lord." That was not an invitation to a dialogue. It was the trumpet of authority, calling us to obedience and freedom and power and glory.[9]

Despite the frustrated allegations of some feminists, God has consistently revealed and portrayed Himself as Father. He identified Himself as the Father of the people of Israel, saying, "Israel is My son, My firstborn."[10] And the feeling was mutual. Repeatedly, the prophets of Israel referred to the Lord as their Father.[11] God said He is the Father of individuals as well as nations.[12] In His mind, no one is to be without a Father, for King David called Him "a father of the fatherless."[13]

God's only begotten Son, Jesus Christ, took on human flesh so that He might reveal and bring us back to the Father. Jesus said that eternal life is wrapped up in knowing God the

Father: "And this is eternal life, that they may know You, the only true God, and Jesus Christ whom You have sent."[14]

When men in postrevolutionary America forsook theology and left the church, they deserted the Judeo-Christian tradition of fatherhood that had given definition to masculinity for all time and eternity. We noted this historic exodus in Chapter 4.

When I say that American men left God, I mean, first of all, that they left the Father. And without the Father in heaven as the anchor of their paternal earthly office, men no longer could determine, with absolute conviction, that the patriarchal role was valid for them to guide their families. Consequently, manhood in America has been tossed about on the seas of continual social change for well over a century and a half.

Historically, God the Father has been called a patriarchal God by all Jews and Christians because He is the source of all things. In spite of post-Christian objections, we cannot escape the fact that as Paul wrote to the church in Corinth, "There is only one God, the Father, of whom are all things."[15]

This is not to say, of course, that God the Son and God the Holy Spirit possess any less of the divine nature than God the Father. You and I equally possess human nature and yet are distinct persons. Likewise, in the blessed Trinity, Father, Son, and Holy Spirit equally possess divine nature and yet are distinct divine persons. One of the things that makes the Father a unique divine person is that He alone is the source of all things.

LET'S GET THEOLOGICAL!

I know I'm getting theological. But men are going to have to get theological—something their passive minds do not want to do—to come back to the truth of manhood. Theology, remember, is a manly discipline. When men forsake the discipline of thinking theologically, they trade the church for commerce and surrender it again to feminine piety. So, rather than just being comfortable and unscholarly, men need to think, even if it hurts.

In the word *patriarchy*, you will recall, *arche* means "first" as well as "to rule." The Father, then, is the first, the fountainhead, the source of all things. Even the other two persons of the Trinity find their eternal source in God the Father, for it is the Father who eternally begets the Son, and it is from the Father that the Holy Spirit eternally proceeds. However, because the Holy Spirit proceeds from the Father, it does not follow that He is less in nature than the Father. It is in their "personness" that the Father, the Son, and the Holy Spirit hold their separate uniqueness.

For instance, the Father is the one unbegotten God. He is unbegotten because no one fathered Him. He alone is the author and source of His own existence, and in this, He is entirely unique. Our earthly father, Adam, images the heavenly Father by being the source of both his wife Eve and his son Seth; that is, Eve proceeded from his side and he beget Seth.

And just as the Holy Spirit is not inferior to the Father in nature, neither is Eve inferior to Adam in human nature. As God the Father is the eternal source of the Son and the Holy Spirit, even so was Adam the source of Eve and Seth.

But more than this, Adam is also the head of this human family in the same way that the Father is the head of the Trinity: the first among equals. In Adam, headship was established in the human race. In Christ, headship is established in the church. And it was to men that God gave, and continues to give, this function. Headship relates to fatherhood and to masculinity. Real men are to be heads of their families.

THE POINT OF GREAT DEBATE

This, of course, is the biblical truth that drives feminists crazy. It is at this point that feminists—male and female,

Christian and non-Christian alike—begin to seethe. It is at this specific point that cries of "chauvinism" are angrily hurled. Failure to bow to this foundational reality in the Scriptures is already producing a whole new generation. It is for this reason that a feminist declaration, "The Document," charges: "Marriage has existed for the benefit of men and has been a legally sanctioned method of control over women . . . the end of the institution of marriage is a necessary condition for the liberation of women."[16]

Why are some people so offended at the idea of male headship that they would call for the abolition of marriage? I am convinced it is due to a gross misunderstanding of the concept of headship, a confusion between a person's value and a person's function.

Headship relates to function. If the male of the species was given the leadership role because he was viewed as innately more valuable, something would indeed be terribly unjust. But giving men the position of family head does not mean that women are of less value than men. Let me try to illustrate this point.

The Chicago Bears won the 1986 Super Bowl. They were led through an incredible season by the National Football League's most valuable coach for 1985, Mike Ditka. In just a few short seasons, Ditka has turned a losing team into a Super Bowl champion. But let me ask you a question: Is Mike Ditka a more valuable human being than the lowliest reserve player on the Bear roster?

Or is President Reagan of greater worth than the Secret Service agent who guards him? Does Lee Iacocca have more innate dignity than the janitor who cleans his office at Chrysler Corporation headquarters? Is *MS.* magazine's Gloria Steinem a more worthy individual than the magazine's newest staff proofreader?

To all of the above, the answer is a resounding no!

A human being's value is not found in *function.* Human worth is described by the phrase *imago Dei,* which means

145

that each of us is made in the image of God. Each person—male or female, rich or poor, famous or obscure—has the same value as the next. No one has any more or any less.

The differences that exist between Mike Ditka and his reserve players, between President Reagan and the Secret Service agent, between Lee Iacocca and the janitor, and between Gloria Steinem and the proofreader having nothing to do with human worth. The differences are not in value, but in function.

In a like manner, the biblically prescribed headship of the husband in human families has nothing to do with men being of greater worth than women, for they are not. The issue is the office or function that God has assigned to each. The failure to differentiate between value and function lies behind much of the power struggle that ravages families across America. Men who actually think they are *more* valuable because God asks them to be the head of the family unit are deceived. And women who feel reduced in personhood because they are not in charge are equally deceived.

To understand this clearly, we have to come back to a true view of God. The perfect model to give us a right understanding of function and value is the Trinity. In the Trinity we find that God the Father is the head, but this headship does not make the Son of less value.

The Father and the Son are equals. The Son is not of less value than the Father because of His function in the Godhead. You see, if function (in Christ's case, of becoming a man) made Him less in value than the Father, He could not be God! But on the contrary, He, according to both the Scriptures and the Nicene Creed, is God of God, Light of Light, the only begotten Son, our Lord Jesus Christ, eternally generated from the Father. *He has no less value because He has a different function.*

LIFE WITH FATHER

Herein lies the answer for those people who are confused by equating function and value. It will put an end to the frantic "climbing of ladders" to prove one's worth. We as human beings are loved by God because we are made by Him. Having been created in His image is the real basis for our worth as persons. Headship, then, does not make one more valuable. Rather, it has been ordained from God the Father, the very source of the blessed Trinity, to assure us of peace, order, and equality.

Without headship, anarchy reigns. Primacy is absolutely necessary for peace in human relationships. Even feminists know this. That's why *Ms.* magazine has an executive editor and why the National Organization for Women has a president.

Headship is essential to the health of the family. As I showed in Chapter 5, since the Victorian era, headship in the American family has been hotly contested. The primary source of tension between American men and women exists because men have left their heavenly model of headship and have ceased to exercise proper leadership in their homes. At best, headship in families is up for grabs. The homes of our land have become battlefields for domestic power struggles. Nevertheless, the ultimate responsibility for decision making within marriages is to be with men.

Why does this sound so unfair to contemporary ears? I believe it is because of the husbands who demand the submission of their wives, but in turn submit to no one themselves! Just as a real man is to be the head of his family, he is also supposed to be under authority himself.

I don't blame the frustrated women who feel the injustice of being under the headship of men who aren't accountable anywhere. It's not fair, and it's also not Christian. Yes, the husband is the head of the wife, but the husband is to be accountable to the leaders of the church. The Scripture says, "Obey those who rule over you, and be submissive, for they watch out for your souls, as those who must give account."[17]

Now that's fair! It is in this relationship that a woman has a court of appeal if she is treated wrongly, which is, by the way, exactly how women were ensured of justice in prerevolutionary America. Colonial women could find justice even in very personal matters; for example, "when one resident of Middlesex County refused to engage in intercourse with his wife for a period of two years, he was excommunicated from the church."[18] Stubborn guys finish last!

There *was* a time when men were accountable for how they treated women. And a patriarchal system provided that accountability.

I have noticed over the last twenty years as I have worked with families that independent men beget independent children who, many times, turn on their parents. Men who are able to function peacefully with a sense of accountability in their own lives, on the other hand, produce children who desire to please them.

Even the Lord Jesus Christ and the Holy Spirit are under the headship of the Father. Therefore, in God the Father we see that headship is a part of fatherhood, while in Christ we see that every other earthly founder and director is under headship himself. Christ is the head of every man because He created man. Yet Christ, while fully sharing the divine nature, is under headship to His Father. In fact, it was this Son, Jesus Christ, who boldly proclaimed, "He who has seen Me has seen the Father; so how can you say, 'Show us the Father'?"[19] In other words, Jesus said to look at Him to see what His Father's patriarchy looked like.

It is imperative that American men understand that Jesus attempted not to destroy or to replace the patriarchal function of men, but to explain its full meaning. His teachings on virginity, equality of the sexes, loving one's enemies, the value of human life, humility, good works, and the absolute sacredness of the marriage bond served to complete the proper patriarchal image of pre-Christian Israel. Jesus came not to abolish patriarchy, but to reveal it. In all honesty, apart from Christ, men will not be adequate fathers. It is only in Him that the fullness of the Father is disclosed.

Being the kind of fathers men are supposed to be means that they must return to patriarchy. Therefore, men should reject the historically inaccurate assertion, so naively believed by Americans of both sexes, that patriarchal families were oppressive families in which women and children suffered at the cruel hands of despotic men. An objective look at the period in American history when patriarchal families were the norm tells just the opposite story. It plainly demonstrates that spouses and children felt far less oppressed and far more content than their modern counterparts.

This antipatriarchal propaganda is part of the Victorian myth that disgraces not only the prerevolutionary colonial family, but the entire Judeo-Christian tradition, whose influence provided family order for the entire world. "Alternative" families are not adequate replacements for traditional families. They are Band-Aids on cancer. Patriarchy is the only workable blueprint for the family. The American home has no chance for survival without it.

11

MARKS OF MANLY LOVE

No one is going to catch me, lady, and make me a
man. I want to be a little boy and to have fun.

Peter Pan[1]

A LOVE THAT INITIATES

There is only one true love: the love of God the Father. But
like two cuts on a diamond, males and females reflect His love
somewhat differently, which is why they need each other. The
first mark of masculine love is that it initiates. How do we
know this? Because as we consider God the Father, who is the
source of all love, we find Him as the prime initiator of love.
He demonstrated this to Jesus Christ His Son when He took
the initiative to proclaim His love to Him by saying: "You are
My beloved Son, in whom I am well pleased."[2]

Jesus acknowledged the Father's primacy of love when He
said, "I have declared to them Your name, and will declare it,
that the love [His Father's love] with which You loved Me may
be in them, and I in them."[3]

The Father moved first toward His Son and then toward His
creation: "God [the Father] so loved the world that He gave
His only begotten Son."[4] And one of Christ's disciples com-
municated that good news—that the Father is the initiator of
love toward us—when he said, "Behold what manner of love

150

the Father has bestowed on us, that we should be called children of God!"[5]

It is written in the Scriptures: "We love Him because He *first* loved us."[6] There is no reason for confusion. Earthly fathers simply must follow the example of God the Father and, by making the first move, initiate acts of love toward their wives, their children, and their friends.

Because love is their responsibility to initiate, and is not dependent upon subjective feelings, men are freed from the tremendous burden of having to wait for the arrival of great emotional intensity before making that first move. By rejecting the disabling voices of passivity and inadequacy, men choose to initiate love whether the emotional desire to do so is present or not. To choose to love and to initiate that love toward people is to act like a man. Because love really is a matter of choice, God can and does command men to initiate it: "Husbands, love your wives, just as Christ also loved the church."[7]

Many men and women are surprised to hear that in the Scriptures husbands are commanded to love their wives unconditionally, but wives are not commanded to love their husbands unconditionally. I have been told that husbands are strongly directed to love because they are more lacking in love than wives. That might be true of modern American men, but this analysis patently does not get to the heart of the divine command.

The commandment to love is given to men because they, like their heavenly Father, are to be initiators of love to fulfill their patriarchal role. But twentieth-century feminized males fail miserably at imitating the Father's example in this regard. Some of them are tragically ignorant of the fact that they are to be the initiators, and others simply do not want to be bothered with the effort that it takes.

As a matter of fact, many men fantasize about women always being the initiators. This compulsive need to be on the receiving end of love is, frankly, one way to check whether a man has been feminized or not. If he finds in himself a need to be pampered and to be propped up by his family and friends and a constant need for approval from others, he doubtless has an extremely difficult time initiating love to others. This is the plight of countless men. A true love, a love that initiates, will powerfully overcome the passivity that paralyzes many men.

A LOVE THAT COMMITS

Patriarchal love also commits. One day in the early seventies, on a sparsely traveled mountain road, a group of twenty young people was returning from an enjoyable outing when one of their cars was involved in an accident in which one of the women passengers was horribly disfigured. What a great tragedy! What was even more tragic than the accident, however, was that the husband of this seriously injured woman, a Christian man, deserted her shortly after the accident. His so-called love failed her at the time of her greatest need. Apparently, that which he called love was not willing to endure the difficult days that would follow.

I don't know what to call such bogus "love." But I do know it is not the committed love that flows from God the Father. Patriarchal love "bears all things."[8] American males who want to act like real men commit themselves to carry the pain of others instead of running away and hiding. Patriarchal love "believes all things, hopes all things."[9] That means that males who want to act like real men commit themselves to faith and to the future.

Probably the most missing element of committed love in today's feminized American male is his willingness to endure all things.[10] Masculine love is strong. It will put up with—even die for—what is right.

The young husband I mentioned earlier had been a fearless

spokesman for Christ on the college campus. But when life's circumstances reduced him to his basic wedding commitment, he flunked the crucial test. He was just another miniature male who, in the wedding ceremony, lied not only to the precious woman he married but also to countless witnesses in heaven and on earth. He became one more pseudomale whose self-centered concept of love could not endure all things.

A LOVE THAT UNIFIES

Men who love are essential to family unity. In the Holy Scriptures, love is called the "bond of perfection."[11] And do the families of this land ever need to be united!

In California, there is a legion of more than seventeen thousand licensed family and marriage therapists. But try as they might, they are fighting a losing war. In just the last decade, despite the efforts of these therapists and their associates nationwide, over twelve million households have been disintegrated by divorce.[12] The nuclear families of America, consisting of a working father, a work-at-home mother, and children, constitute a pathetic 7 percent of all U.S. households.[13] The rate at which American families are falling apart has prompted Columbia University sociology professor Amatae Etzione to state, "We can no longer consider the total breakdown of the family as inconceivable."[14]

Where has family unity gone? And more important, who should be holding this most indispensable of social units together? The family is falling apart because fathers are failing to fulfill their patriarchal roles as unifiers.

Fathers who aren't manly enough to take responsible action to preserve the unity of their homes will ultimately live in chaos. What kind of leader allows turmoil to ruin his country? As much as most Americans hate both communism and fascism, there is one condition worse than all—anarchy. When anarchy reigns, everybody loses.

What pastor lets his church continue in discord and up-heaval over one unruly brother? What teacher allows an un-cooperative student to continually distract the entire class? Yet feminized American men have stood by as anarchy ripped apart their homes. To come to true manhood is to be a source of unity. American men are responsible for the unity of their families, and it is from that unity that peace and order flow.

A LOVE THAT SACRIFICES

Another mark of authentic manhood that American males desperately need to recover is the willingness to sacrifice for the sake of righteousness. Sacrifice! What a rare word in to-day's self-fulfillment society.

Every day men are bombarded with countless messages ex-tolling the virtues of self-gratification. From Burger King's invitation to "Have it your way" to Michelob's promise that "You can have it all," men are continually being seduced into putting themselves first. Millions of American men have been lulled into a lifestyle in which virtually every moment of their discretionary time is spent in the pursuit of self-centered ac-tivities.

From professional obligations, to leisure activities, to com-munity and charitable pursuits, the involvement of men seems predicated on the amount of self-fulfillment that any given activity might return to them. What can *I* get out of it? is the question voiced much too frequently. Activities and re-lationships that once existed primarily for the benefit of oth-ers are quickly dropped if they do not give men a heightened sense of personal fulfillment.

In the forty-plus years I have been in the church, I have no-ticed the increasing frequency with which Christians switch churches. The move to a new congregation is usually made because the church left behind was "not feeding me"—as if the primary purpose of Christian worship and service was to fill personal needs. Even families are not exempt from this love affair with self. High on the list of reasons the typical American male gives for dumping his wife and children is that he was not having his needs met.

The hesitancy to sacrifice time and personal pleasure lies in sharp contrast to the spirit of sacrifice seen in the lives of godly men throughout history. These men willingly made great sacrifices because it was the right thing to do. Abraham had to sacrifice his homeland. So willing was he to sacrifice to do God's will that he was willing to sacrifice the life of his only son, Isaac, whom he deeply loved.

Moses sacrificed family, wealth, and the very throne of Egypt to do God's will. Space does not allow me to mention those who made the *ultimate* sacrifice—the countless men since Moses who were fed to lions, sawed in two, and burned at the stake for the sake of righteousness. Stephen had to sacrifice his life for the sake of the gospel of Christ. He is called the protomartyr of the church, the first to die for his faith. But Jesus stood up to welcome him home!

And as in everything pertaining to being a good father, the supreme example of the willingness to sacrifice is seen in God the Father. Can you imagine willingly sending your only son to die a torturous death in order to ransom the very people who would inflict such atrocities on him? But this is the sacrifice that God the Father made on our behalf.

Historically, before traditional masculinity evaporated from the American scene, the willingness to sacrifice for righteousness' sake was viewed as a normal part of being a man. The colonial man was willing to sacrifice any personal time he might have had in order to do what was right for his family. Although there were normal times of recreation, the term *vacation* was unheard of, and the concept of retirement was completely unknown. The man's life, and even his free time, revolved around what was best for his family until the day he died.

155

Today, having "my own space" is deemed an inalienable right by many men. But if men want to do what is right for their families, they must be willing to sacrifice. And the first thing up for grabs is free time. If a man spends all his available moments in front of the television and video playback unit, in four different softball leagues, or in a bar, how can he expect his children to become anything but self-absorbed individuals?

Real men know that their days of childhood, when responsibilities were few and leisure time was plentiful, are gone. Patriarchal men are committed to give themselves up for the sake of righteousness, to sacrifice for their wives, their children, and their friends.

A LOVE THAT IS ZEALOUS

Another mark of authentic manhood, which I've never seen mentioned in the "touchy-feely" books about men, is zeal. A truly masculine man is unashamedly zealous for his family. Today, a zealous person is usually suspiciously looked upon as one who gets a little carried away, a fanatic who is obsessed and out of control. To refer to someone as a zealot is to consider him a well-intentioned fool, a good man who doesn't know when to stop.

What a contrast this is to our model for manhood! Zeal is one of the most noticeable characteristics of God the Father. Over and over again, zeal is an attribute used to describe Him. Our God is a zealous God. And what is the object of His zeal? His beloved people. Repeatedly, God said of the people of Zion, "I am zealous for Zion with great zeal; / With great fervor I am zealous for her."[15]

This Father's zeal is an ardent, intense, fervent, even passionate concern for the welfare of His children. At times, God's zeal for Israel made Him act like a man of war.[16] His zeal brought them out of captivity in foreign lands.[17] And His zeal for them led to His sending Jesus Christ to be the Messiah.[18]

God's zeal always had a purpose. It was aimed at keeping His people together. Even when He had to punish them for their disobedience, God always saw that a remnant survived so the family could remain intact. God was zealous for the stability of His family.

In the early seventies, Vance Packard authored a best seller called *A Nation of Strangers*. From his study of relationships in American culture, he found us to be "a cold society." And one of the major problems that turned the thermostat down on the relationships between American neighbors was mobility. Approximately 25 percent of the population in the United States is constantly on the move.

By contrast, as we look at the actions of God the Father throughout biblical history, we see His zeal is aimed at *gathering* His people, keeping them intact. The more than one million people of Israel who came out of Egypt under Moses' leadership were organized into communities and family groupings—the theme of the book of Numbers. The tribe of Levi, the tribe of Judah, the tribe of Simeon—they were all born into their own families.

"Those families of Israel *knew* where they fit, too," writes Richard Ballew. He continues:

> They didn't wander around like nomads among other families; they knew where they were to brush their teeth and comb their hair. They knew where they were to eat their meals. They were cared for. And they were related to one another on the basis of a law which said, "You shall love the Lord your God with all your heart, soul, mind and strength. And you shall love your neighbor as yourself." Sounds like a solution to the identity crisis, doesn't it? You relate to God, you relate to yourself and you also relate to your neighbor.[19]

But this can happen only with family heads who are zealous to make it happen—men who take their cues from their heavenly Father, men who give priority to the well-being of their wives and children.

Manly zeal aimed toward fatherly responsibilities will ultimately produce a healthy society. Everyone will benefit. Young mothers will be assisted during the energy-consuming days of child rearing by grandparents, uncles, and aunts who understand their roles. Regaining this normal and historical relationship will be rough on the growing phenomenon of child-care centers, but it will certainly be great for the children.

Elderly grandparents will be useful and respected as they keep their lives properly involved in the welfare of the family. This might be rough on rest homes, motor home sales, and retirement village developers in Arizona, but it will surely give a rich blessing to the elderly instead of loneliness in their later years. The extended family will not be good for singles bars, single encounter groups, or adults-only apartments, but unmarried people will overcome loneliness, lack of self-worth, and the vulnerability that haunts them as they regain their dignity and protection by contributing and relating to the family.

The American family is in the midst of a battle for its existence. It is being attacked on every front, and nothing will save it apart from God the Father and men who follow His example. These men embrace zeal as a part of their manhood because they see the zeal of a patriarchal God for His people and want to be like Him.

A LOVE THAT MODELS

One of the most ignored fathers of all time has to be Joseph, the earthly father of Jesus. The Scriptures state that he was a "righteous" man, and because he was a righteous man, he was a model Jesus could safely follow.

Joseph protected his family by departing to Egypt, thus

avoiding the slaughter of thousands of baby boys by Herod the king. Joseph, with his wife Mary, went to Jerusalem to offer a sacrifice and to present their first-born child to the heavenly Father. Under the headship of Joseph, Jesus grew strong and wise—strong, because He imitated His father Joseph's trade of carpentry, and wise, because His earthly father was a man of wisdom who had the grace of God upon him.

Joseph took his family to the Feast of the Passover in Jerusalem every year. And, yes, Joseph—like all fathers who err from time to time—left for the trip back to Nazareth without Jesus. When Joseph realized what had happened at the end of a day's journey, he and Mary turned back immediately to Jerusalem. They found Jesus in the temple, and Mary said to Him, "Son, why have You done this to us? Look, Your *father* and I have sought You anxiously."[20]

Sounds like a mother, doesn't it? Mary was referring to the concern of His earthly father, Joseph. Jesus answered her question by saying, "Did you not know that I must be about My Father's business?"[21] Did He mean that from that time He would relate only to His heavenly Father and not to His earthly parents anymore? Not at all. Following this event, the biblical account notes that He "was subject to them" and that He "increased in wisdom and stature, and in favor with God and men."[22]

Was Jesus following Joseph or God? It wasn't an either-or situation for Him, nor should it be for us. It is both. For Jesus, to follow Joseph's example *was* to walk in the will of His heavenly Father. It is the same for all children who seek to obey the Father of their fathers.

What does that say to fathers? It could change their lives and especially their relationships with their children. The reason youths are following artificial media models like Boy George and Rambo, the reason this generation of teen-agers resurrects James Dean, the old rebel model of my high-school days, and the reason the tragic life of Elvis Presley has been canonized in the minds of American youths is that fathers are no longer models for their children.

WHERE THE RUBBER MEETS THE ROAD

So what do men do? I know what I did. I sat down with my son and told him that he didn't have to chase after phony models who didn't know him, who didn't belong to him, who didn't care about him. All he needed to do was to be like me. Egotistic? Not on your life. Risky? Absolutely! But I established our relationship the way it was meant to be. Does that mean a man has to be perfect? No. It just means that he better have a heart for what is right.

I make mistakes, but I also repent. If my son imitates me in that, he will be fine. Children really do want to be like their fathers. I wrestled in high school. My son wrestled in high school. I like to draw. My son likes to draw. I like dirt bikes. My son likes dirt bikes. Does that mean that I'm trying to make my son into a little clone of myself? No. That is not the issue here. There are numerous things about my son that are markedly different from the way I'm put together.

What it does mean is that my son is going to believe what I believe. If he doesn't, I can count on his believing what someone else believes. Some readers may protest, "You mean you're going to tell your son what to believe?" I most certainly am.

If fathers cannot do that, they are doing their sons a great disservice. They need to change their attitudes. Or they need to change what they believe. Because my children had a model, my son, who is eighteen, and my daughter who is nineteen, never had to struggle with "finding the will of God." This may offend some people, but the will of God for my children is to do the will of their father and mother until they marry and begin families of their own. That is why the Bible says, "Children, obey your parents in the Lord."[23] How that uncomplicates the lives of children in the midst of a complicated society!

What about the children's identity? Does such obedience not tend to destroy their identity as persons?

Let me ask this: Did the identity of our Lord Jesus Christ suffer because He imitated His Father? Hardly. He was the most balanced, well-adjusted man who ever walked the earth.

Dr. James Dobson, well-known author and Christian counselor, said in a film on Christian fathering, "Dad was not only my very good friend—my father, of course—but also my partner. Nearly everything I write originated in a conversation with him."[24]

In the effort to recover responsible manhood, fathers must declare themselves the models for their sons. That is the normal relationship that brings boys to manhood. It is part and parcel of true patriarchal fatherhood. The apostle Paul boldly declared this truth to an entire church when he said, "For in Christ Jesus I have begotten you through the gospel. Therefore I urge you, imitate me."[25]

Years ago, our family was returning from a trip to Idaho where we had been visiting friends. As we wound up and through the mountains just out of Pocatello, the snow became increasingly deeper on the edge of the roads. It appeared that we were in an area where no one else had ever lived, but out of the corner of my eye, I saw an old wooden schoolhouse perched on a secluded hill. It was probably built at the turn of the century.

I'm a sucker for old things. I'm enraptured by old barns and especially old schoolhouses. Grabbing the camera, I jumped out of the car and began the ascent up the hill through the deep snow.

As I approached the weather-beaten school, my mind was trying to visualize the children whose feet carried them to

161

these doors. Suddenly, I heard a frantic cry from behind me. About thirty yards down the hill, a little head popped out of a snowbank. It was my then-six-year-old son, stuck in a drift. I didn't know he had followed me.

When I went down the hill to rescue him, he sobbed, "Your steps got too far apart. I couldn't jump in your feet anymore."

The young people of America—its sons—really do desire to follow somebody. Just as my son wanted to do, the footsteps that sons want to walk in are those belonging to their fathers. Tragically, millions of fathers have bought the damaging propaganda that it's wrong to want their sons to be like them. Still others, like the inferior Victorian man, feel hopelessly inadequate to model masculinity.

To be masculine is to be willing to be a model of love. And unless men commit themselves to imitate their heavenly Father and become models for their own sons, their boys will have an even tougher time becoming real men than they have had.

They have a choice before them. Like Peter Pan, they can continue to act like boys and refuse to grow up. But if they continue to choose that option, they can look forward to suffering even more terrible and dramatic consequences than they have already witnessed.

Or they can respond to the words of the apostle Paul and act like men by imitating God the Father in His patriarchal ways. Only when men are willing to imitate the Father's love—a love that initiates, commits, unifies, sacrifices, is full of zeal, and models—will they learn what it means to be mature men.

12

RETURNING TO MANHOOD

Fight the good fight of faith.

The apostle Paul[1]

The pain was excruciating. He knew he was badly injured. Most boxers would have thrown in the towel, but he kept coming back.

For seven more rounds he ignored the incredible pain in his abdomen and chest and continued to exchange a flurry of blows with his opponent. His tenacity paid off. At the end of the fight, the referee raised his right hand in victory. After the match, though, he quickly disappeared behind the barracks. Wrapping his aching arms around his burning chest, he began to vomit blood until he thought he would die.

Some would say this scrappy little army fighter refused to quit because the guest of honor at the exhibition match that day at Fort Lewis, Washington, was none other than General George Patton. But I know better. Had no one but his opponent been there, Dad would have boxed with the same dogged determination. My father was a fighter.

When I was eleven, I was rummaging through some dresser drawers, and I unearthed the old boxing medal. It was then that I first heard the story of this fight. I can't begin to tell you the impact my father's victory had on my life. But it was

163

not the blow-by-blow and round-by-round description of the fight that made the lasting impression on me.

"You know," Dad said, "if measured by pain and suffering, I lost that fight. But the record book says I won. I succeeded because of only one thing. I had a fighting heart. Son, you won't achieve anything in life without a fighting heart."

I have never forgotten his words. Somehow, in that brief, rare moment, I decided that my goals in life were not going to be sabotaged by the prospects of pain. I was not going to let the desire for comfort and pleasure be the controlling force of my decisions. Most of all, I was not going to be passive. I was going to fight.

Let me be quick to say that I don't mean I decided to be contentious and quarrelsome, a man who loves a fight because he is pugnacious—something the Scriptures condemn. What I am saying is that I'm committed to fight for those values in life that, when fulfilled, produce godly, responsible masculinity.

No matter how you slice it, life is a battle. And men who refuse to fight will end up trampled underfoot by those who care enough to put their time and energy where their mouth is. Since life is a struggle, why not fight for what is right? The apostle Paul called that "the good fight."

If men fight for what is right, it doesn't matter if a thousand demonic voices are predicting the annihilation of the family and advocating a requiem for fatherhood. Frankly, I've had it with the prophets of paternal doom. I'm tired of men standing on the sidelines while their wives have become the sole moral instructors of the children. I'm tired of the men of America finding more satisfaction in watching television than in watching out for the welfare of their families. I'm through watching television documentaries on the "hopeless plight" of young American black men that provide them with no answers. Frankly, I'm tired of seeing Americans trying to define man without God. Here are some things that I think need to be done.

WHAT SOCIETY CAN DO

The Government

American government usually takes action on issues that have an impact on the lives of large numbers of its citizens. I was reminded of this the other day when I entered a restaurant and was asked whether I wanted to be seated in the smoking or nonsmoking section of the establishment. Because of concern over the effects of cigarette smoking, the government of my home state of California requires smokers to sit in a separate area. The federal government, because of the same concern, forbids radio, television, and billboard advertising peddling cigarettes and even requires manufacturers to print health warnings on every pack of cigarettes. This is appropriate action. Too many American families have had to deal with the anguish of smoking-related diseases. But even *greater* numbers of Americans have had their lives wrecked by the actions and inactions of irresponsible men. The government has rightly taken action to deal with the first problem. It has failed almost completely to undertake any action on the second problem.

Surely, the same government that warns the populace that smoking is dangerous to health can also warn the men of America that abandoning their homes is extremely dangerous to the health of our entire nation. Government can do more than exhort through proclamation. It can create laws that pressure men to act responsibly. It can put a lot more teeth into child-support laws. It can enact legislation that would truly make divorce the action of last resort instead of the action of first option. It can change welfare laws so that men find it more economically attractive to stay with their families and work than it is to leave them and not work. It can give able-bodied, unemployed men dignity by providing them jobs that allow them—indeed, even require them—to work for welfare money.

Government needs to do a lot more than it presently does to

call males back to responsible manhood. Manhood is a resource we must not forget.

The Schools

Government is not the only American social institution that
can help call men back to responsible action. There is much
that the educators of our children can do as well.

Earlier, I tried to demonstrate that schoolboys fare far
worse than their female counterparts because the elementary
schools of America are extremely feminized. What can be
done to alleviate the problem? I can offer several suggestions
that would help immensely.

First, we need more men teachers in elementary education.
When I ask educators why men constitute only 17 percent of
all elementary teachers, they tell me that most men believe
that elementary education is the domain of women. Dr. J. W.
Rollings of the California Department of Education attributes the lack of male teachers in the elementary school to this
same "societal stereotyping." In other words, men still buy
the Victorian myth that women possess an innate moral superiority that better qualifies them to educate the minds of
impressionable children. Be assured, our boys will continue
to flounder if we perpetuate this lie any longer.

In addition, the educators of America should consider re-
structuring elementary curricula to also allow for the masculine modes of learning that currently have little or no place in
elementary schools today. We should allow more time for
boys to learn how to play and develop social skills before we
emphasize academic skills. In fact, studies show that coun-
tries where educators begin giving academic instruction
much later than we do experience a significantly lower rate of
learning maladies.

Now the corker! I am convinced that the changes necessary
to secure male and female identities in elementary education
could best be accomplished by sex-separated classrooms. If

that makes you chuckle or gasp, tell me why people who have the economic means to provide the best education possible for their children so often choose sex-segregated private schools or academies? And why are these the schools that produce the leaders, male and female, of this nation in numbers far disproportionate to other schools their size?

Finally, for the sake of justice, educators at all levels must make the study of masculinity a subject that is given the same attention as women's studies.

The Church

The church in modern America has been anemic and, in some instances, downright impotent as a force for moral guidance in our culture. It is time for the Christian churches to free the feminized men of America from Victorian piety. The state and the school can only do so much in calling men to responsible manhood. Ultimately, the return to manhood is not a matter of government proclamation or educational policy as much as it is a spiritual matter.

Thus, the Christian church is in the unique position of being able to give the ultimate answers that men need to hear. The church alone can point to the one perfect model. Therefore, it is critical that those who preach a "Jesus only" or a "Jesus and Holy Spirit only" gospel return to an orthodox, or right, view of God the Father. The Father must be worshiped and honored together with the Son and the Holy Spirit.

It is imperative that American men, through the illumination of the Holy Spirit, have their eyes opened to see the Father-Son relationship. And it is the church's responsibility to make these truths clearly known so that men can understand their masculinity and know what it means to be fathers.

Men must be built up in Christ and re-established in church leadership. For too long the church has compromised, accommodated, and at times surrendered to the spirit of this age.

167

Presently, the church is not only intimidated by, but is caving in further to, a fresh revival of Victorian feminism.

The church must return to the moral front of protest. And one sure place to begin is to protest the current emasculation of American men. For once, let's see the church on the prophetic cutting edge.

One place to start is by defeminizing the Sunday schools for our boys. It is no secret that thousands of young males leave the church each year—many of them for good. One of the reasons, if not *the* leading cause, for this desertion is the female-dominated Sunday school. The church must not make the same mistake made by the public schools. It must set the pace by having men teach young boys in the masculine ways that turn them on to the church.

WHAT INDIVIDUALS CAN DO

I have committed myself to fight, to rediscover the responsibilities of true manhood. I hope other men will, too. Here are the specific goals I am committed to pursue to guard and strengthen my own responsibilities as a husband and father. I believe these areas of concern relate to all men.

1. Authentic Fathers

The first step men need to make is to commit themselves to authentic fatherhood, to take the initiative in restoring stability and peace to the suffering homes of the land. But this can only happen when men are willing to stop whimpering about their wants, needs, and desires and pay the price of sacrificing time and energy for the well-being of their families and the oppressed and neglected in their communities.

They need to tell the irresponsible Pied Pipers of self-indulgence to take a hike. A return to authentic fatherhood demands that men abandon their preoccupation with self-fulfillment and self-gratification.

Authentic fatherhood calls upon the men of America to

stop being nice and start being truthful—to do what is right for their wives and children, no matter what the cost.

2. Followers of God the Father

The return to fatherhood will not endure the test of time unless it is established on a sure foundation. It must be built on a foundation of truth rather than wishful thinking. Therefore, above anything else, Christian men must commit themselves to the care and guidance of God the Father. If men are ever going to figure out who they are supposed to be, it is imperative that they know the very source of their existence: the one true Patriarch.

It is my observation, based on personal involvement, that the Jesus movement and the charismatic movement of the last two decades awoke many of the men of America to a long-dormant spiritual sensitivity. But these men were still confused about who they were. Much confusion was added to their lives as they tried to adopt feminine characteristics in worship that put too much value on emotion. Trying to "keep the high," many burned out. In fact, never have so many "Christian" marriages of both leaders and laymen gone on the rocks as since the time of both the Jesus movement and the charismatic movement. Whatever good came out of these events, they did not seem to bring about the very thing both Jesus and the Holy Spirit intend to accomplish.

Jesus said, "But the hour is coming, and now is, when the true worshipers will worship *the Father* in spirit and truth; for the Father is seeking such to worship Him."[2]

Christ as the Son of God gives full obedience to the Father while being of one nature with the Father. And the Holy Spirit is also related. Jesus said that the Holy Spirit "proceeds from the Father"[3] and that the Holy Spirit is the promise of the Father[4] who came at Pentecost. The incarnate Son of God and the Holy Spirit were sent by God the Father to bring mankind back to Himself.

Therefore, men must not only commit themselves to the lordship of Jesus Christ or be filled with the Holy Spirit. They must learn to know and worship God the Father. They must know all three persons of the holy Trinity. As men commit themselves to follow the heavenly Father, their lives, their identity, their families, and the nation will begin to be healed!

3. Churchmen

When Jesus found the wayward merchants making the house of God a place of commerce, He made a whip of cords, drove them out of the temple, overturned their money tables, and said, "Take these things away! Do not make My Father's house a house of merchandise!"[5] The Son is zealous for His Father's house.

That is the manly zeal American men must regain toward the Father's house—the church. That's right—the church. Not some counterfeit do-gooder organization or some country club for the religious folk. It is in the church that the triune God reigns.

Don't the Holy Scriptures teach that Christ "loved the church and gave Himself for it"?[6] In the church men can submit their lives to the lordship of Christ and regain the stability they were created to possess. In the church Christ ensures that men have earthly models of fatherhood. Ignatius, the early bishop of Antioch, wrote in A.D. 107 that "all are to respect the deacons as Jesus Christ and the bishop as a copy of the Father."[7]

The church must be the priority for the men of America.

4. Men True Until Death

Men must commit themselves to their wives and families unto death. Only this kind of commitment will enable the family to survive the life-and-death struggle for existence. Besides, that is what good men do. A good shepherd lays down his life for the sheep and does not flee when he sees trouble coming.

As I write this, my secretary has informed me that a sixty-year-old friend of hers has just left his wife of thirty-four years "for better sex." Can you believe it? It's time for men to turn up the heat of disapproval toward any of their brothers who even think about abandoning faithful wives.

I heard of another fellow who left his wife for another woman because of "lack of intimacy." How feminized, how subjective are men going to get? Marriage is a sacrament! It was the purpose of God to establish one man with one woman for one lifetime. A husband and a wife are to become one flesh, and their marriage is to last their entire lives. Jesus said, " 'And the two shall become one flesh'; so then they are no longer two, but one flesh. Therefore what God has joined together, let not man separate.'"[8]

I can remember how frightened I was at twenty-two years of age to commit myself for life to my wife. The palms of my hands even broke out in a sweat when I purchased the rings. I was rightly fearful. It's a serious thing to make a covenant before God and witnesses that you are going to stick with the woman who is your wife—no matter what. It takes courage, does it not, to remain faithful when the "what" comes? But the promise is already made, and God gives mercy through marriage to keep the promise. We have no excuse to go back on that promise. The prophet Malachi announced that God "hates divorce."[9] That means to me that men who are made in the image of God must hate divorce as well.

5. Virgin Bachelors

The commitments I am calling for are not just for men with wives and families. The single men of America need to commit themselves to spiritual fatherhood, and they would do well to remain virgin in singleness. With real men, virginity is "in"—not promiscuity. And it takes an unintimidated man of courage to take that stand in the midst of a sexually preoccupied society.

In the city of San Francisco, over 1,000 single men have died from AIDS, 42 of them in a 30-day period. And 101 new cases surfaced in those same 30 days. Predictions say it is going to get worse; the federal government forecasts that more people will die from AIDS in 1991 than will die in automobile accidents that year. What will stop this calamity? Virginity.

There are good reasons to refrain from sex before marriage. Premarital sex builds mistrust. One reason husbands and wives are able to trust each other is that they waited to have sex until they were married. And people who waited thank God they did. What they learned during that time of self-discipline and waiting was that if they could wait then, they could also refrain if they were tempted after they got married. Sexual purity builds trust.

Marriages will joyfully endure the test of time again when single men commit themselves to entering into marriage clean, rather than bringing with them sexual memories from the past. That is what fathers must commit themselves to want for their sons and daughters, also. That's what the white dress is all about at the wedding—a symbol of virginity come true. Such purity will be costly, and it will take the steadfast commitment of real men. But the benefits, individually and socially, will be worth it. The old cliché—Lust can't wait to get, but love can wait to give—isn't a bad one after all.

6. Role Models for Sons

American men must again become models for their sons. This means they must live godly lives and admit it when they fail. My experience in working with men today, and I'm speaking of Christian men, is that they are afraid to ask their own sons to imitate them. They reject the example of the apostle Paul, who speaking as a father to his children in the faith said, "I urge you, imitate me."[10]

The famous British prime minister, Winston Churchill, who pursued a career in Parliament as his father before him, wrote,

The greatest and most powerful influence in my early life was of course my father. Although I had talked with him so seldom and never for a moment on equal terms, I conceived an intense admiration and affection for him; and after his early death, for his memory. I read industriously almost every word he had ever spoken and learnt by heart large portions of his speeches. I took my politics almost unquestioningly from him. . . . He seemed to own the key to everything or almost everything worth having.[11]

Like you and me, Churchill's father was far less than a flawless man. But his lack of perfection did not disqualify him as a model. A look at the way that Winston turned out shows that we don't have to be perfect to be adequate models for our sons. Men must call their sons to follow them as they follow Christ.

7. Pursuers of Virtue

When was the last time you heard men discussing virtue as a manly thing to pursue? Virtue links masculinity with moral excellence. *Vir* in Latin literally means "a man," not in a general sense of the entire human race, but specifically "a male." And the Latin *virtus* can mean "strength," "manliness," or "moral perfection."

In other words, though women are to be virtuous, don't think for a moment that virtue is only an adornment meant for women. Men have only two alternatives by which to walk: virtue or vice. Therefore, men need to willingly clothe themselves with a mantle of virtue because only virtue produces the true objective of being responsible to both God and man. And a man who wants to complete his manhood and image God the Father will seek virtue like a pearl hidden in a field.

8. Real Men Say No

Based on my own observations, I would say that American men have a greater problem with being too submissive than

173

with being too aggressive. That is, they say yes when they should say no. Men give in to pressures and promises when they shouldn't, especially when they think giving in will bring them some good feelings or happiness.

A friend of mine has made the following observation:

> Happiness became the dream of a nation. Our constitution assumes that all men desire "life, liberty, and the pursuit of happiness." Ironically the assumption of the right of happiness has brought great misery in our day. A man will divorce his wife because she cannot make him happy. A woman will abort her child because the child might violate her right to happiness. Children have brought suits against their parents because they were robbed of a happy childhood. Any action can be justified by "I was not happy."[12]

When happiness becomes an idol, it becomes very hard to say no to things that should be rejected. Men need to relearn the manly art of saying no. Who knows how many marriages have gone down the drain because men, obsessed with some false concept of happiness, have not had the responsible courage to say that one little word? No!—to the big corporation that promises the "nice" increase in salary if a man will tear his wife away from her needed friends, yank his children from familiar schools, chop off the ties with the church, and uproot all community relationships. No!—to the committee that wants the last free night of a man's week for some "good cause" if it means being with his family is no longer possible. No!—to the young man who wants to live with his daughter rather than work out a proper courtship that leads to marriage. No!—to the flattering eyes of the adulteress.

Emphatically, with both feet planted firmly on the ground, men must commit themselves to saying no to things, good or bad, that would take them away from their patriarchal responsibility to make Christ and His kingdom the critical priority.

9. Gentlemen

America needs *gentlemen* again. I don't mean by that word stuffy, overly proper knaves who are obsessed with rules of etiquette. I mean men who bring honor to their own homes and communities by giving honor to others.

The very origin of the word *gentleman* calls for a man who cares about his family and how he represents them to the rest of the world. *Gentle* literally means "belonging to the same family." It does not mean "soft" or "bland." The name *gentleman* gives the proper—and maybe *only*—alternative to the false macho or weakling stereotypes of today's American culture. Gentlemen are family men, men who worship God and respect other men and women because they have been created in His image.

10. One of the Boys

Masculinity is re-enforced and feminization can be overcome by men spending time with other men. I am astonished at how many men have been so affected by the feminizing forces that have moved through our culture that they feel uncomfortable with other men and prefer the company of women.

Many men I talk with do not have a close male friend, a "buddy." Their wives, they like to proclaim, are their "best friends." My wife *is* my dear friend, but she can never replace—nor would she care to replace—my strong male comrades. Male companionship helps clarify male characteristics.

Throughout history, men have always come together to "say" or "do" things common to the male gender. That kind of comradeship is healthy for men, and it goes a long way in teaching and reminding men about who they are. I have personally found that having a "night out with the boys" is the most relaxing time for me. In fact, sometimes when I am getting grumpy around the house, my wife will say, "Why don't you go out with some of the guys tonight?" It benefits the whole family for me to share in male companionship.

My wife has learned that my time with other men has not hindered our marriage; rather, it has helped it! It is in that context that men can let go a bit and not have to carry the responsibility required of them in all the other areas of their lives. That time lets them regroup and refresh their vision to be the men they need to be.

What about rounding up some of the guys for a night out at the ballpark? Or a relaxed conversation over a big steak? Or a double-elimination round of bowling? Men need to commit themselves to making a place for male companionship.

BACK IN THE BATTLE!

Centuries ago, ten years past his hundredth birthday, one of Israel's greatest leaders grouped the people of God together for what turned out to be his farewell address. He presented them to God and rehearsed with them all the things God had done for them.

He talked boldly with them about their tendencies to serve other gods. Then he brought them to a point of decision. It's God or gods, he warned them. And he laid down a challenge that is so powerful in its simplicity that it still rings through the consciousness of our churches and our homes. It is quoted in sermons and on greeting cards, and it is etched upon gilded plaques. "As for me and for my house," Joshua proclaimed, "we will serve the LORD."[13]

Isn't the Lord facing men with that same option today? God the Father exhorts men to act like men, to take their place as heads of their homes and choose with their wives and children to follow Him. The gods of this age—passivity, fatigue, indecision, feminization—beg men to cave in and follow them. But men of God must choose another course.

Let the resolve of Joshua sound forth loud and clear as it calls the men of America back to responsible manhood. Let it sound with such power that it stirs to action the hearts of men from the sidewalks of New York, to the lakeshore of Chicago, to the wheatfields of Nebraska, to the cliffs of California. It is a call to men of every race, a call to men of every economic status.

Men should make their choice this moment. They cannot be content to just think about it. Men must decide for the God of their fathers. For too long, they have believed the arrogant lies of modernity that newer is better, that a break with tradition is for the best, that patriarchal is passé.

The call is a battle cry. It beckons men to war. Hordes of prejudiced critics will mount an attack, a counteroffensive to stop the return of men to historical and biblical patterns of manhood. Men must be committed to the foundational fatherhood upon which all civilizations have been built and must now be reconstructed.

Godly, virtuous, male leadership has been missing for too many generations in America. It is time for the men of America to return to the front lines of responsibility. Men must get back to the action, where they belong!

NOTES ──────────────────────────────

Chapter 1—The Death of Masculinity

1. Myron Brenton, *The American Male* (New York: Coward-McCann, 1966), 13.
2. Elaine Partnow, ed., *The Quotable Woman*, 2 vols. (Los Angeles: Pinnacle Books, 1977), 2:252.
3. The figures that follow are a general compilation of government statistics.
4. *Introducing the University* (Berkeley: Office of the Assistant V.P.—Student Academic Services, UCB, 1985–86).
5. *University of California Santa Cruz General Catalog* (Santa Cruz, Calif.: UCSC Publication, 1984), 246.
6. Ibid., 233–38.
7. Ann Landers, "Daddy Was A Wimp," *Santa Cruz Sentinel*, October 25, 1984, B-5.

Chapter 2—Four False Icons

1. Jerry Mander, *Four Arguments for the Elimination of Television* (New York: Quill, 1978), 239.
2. Joan Mellen, *Big Bad Wolves* (New York: Pantheon Books, 1977), vii.
3. David Ansen, "An American Icon," *Newsweek*, July 22, 1985, 50.
4. Mellen, *Bad Wolves*, vii.
5. Diane O'Connor and Dick O'Connor, *How to Make Your Man More Sensitive* (New York: Dutton, 1975), 3.
6. Mike Wallace, "Carroll O'Connor answers the tough questions about 'Archie Bunker,'" *Good Housekeeping*, October 1974, 200.

7. Edwin Louis Cole, *Maximized Manhood* (Springdale, Penn.: Whitaker House, 1984), 127.
8. Maurice Horn, *The World Encyclopedia of Comics* (New York: Chelsea House, 1976), 118–19.
9. Brenton, *American Male*, 142.
10. Marshall Hamilton, *Father's Influence on Children* (Chicago: Nelson-Hall, 1979), citing LeMaster.
11. David Manning White and Robert H. Abel, *The Funnies* (London: Collier-Macmillan, 1963), 180.
12. Natalie Gittelson, *Dominus* (New York: Farrar, Straus & Giroux, 1978), 23.
13. Giora Dilibeto, "Invasion of the Gender Blenders," *People*, April 23, 1984, 97.
14. Steven Simels, *Gender Chameleons* (New York: Timbre Books/Arbor House, 1985), 19.
15. Ibid., 35.
16. Dilibeto, "Gender Blenders," 99.
17. Kathleen Beckett, "The Menswear Phenomenon," *Vogue*, August 1984, 164.
18. Dilibeto, "Gender Blenders," 99.
19. John Leo, "The Eleventh Megatrend," *Time*, July 23, 1984, 104.
20. Nicholas Jennings, "Blurring the Boundaries of Gender," *Macleans*, July 23, 1984, 44.
21. Alvin Toffler, *The Third Wave* (Toronto: Bantam Books, 1982), 123, italics added.
22. Ibid.
23. Ibid., 123, 124.
24. Ray Zell, "Revision or Perversion: An Attempt to De-Sex the Scriptures," *Again*, vol. 7, no. 1, 18.

Chapter 3—When Manhood Came to America

1. Mary P. Ryan, *Womanhood in America* (New York: Franklin Watts, 1983), 67.
2. Ibid., 21.
3. Peter N. Stearns, *Be A Man* (New York: Holmes & Meier, 1979), 28.
4. Edmund S. Morgan, *Virginians at Home* (New York: Holt, Rinehart & Winston, 1952), 45.
5. Stearns, *Be A Man*, 26.
6. Ann Douglas, *The Feminization of American Culture* (New York: Knopf, 1977), 6.
7. Ryan, *Womanhood*, 67.
8. Morgan, *Virginians*, 44.
9. Ibid.
10. Frank Freidel, *Changing Ideas About Women in the United States, 1776–1825* (New York: Garland, 1981), 8.
11. James Dobson, *What Wives Wish Their Husbands Knew About Women* (Wheaton Ill.: Tyndale, 1975), 22.
12. Ryan, *Womanhood*, 31.
13. Ibid., 38.

14. Dobson, *What Wives Wish*, 59.
15. Ryan, *Womanhood*, 35.
16. Smith, *Daughters of the Promised Land*, 43–44.
17. Ibid., 47.
18. Smith, *Daughters of the Promised Land*, 45.
19. Morgan, *Virginians*, 50.
20. Gregg Lewis, "The Return of Apathy," *Christianity Today*, October 18, 1985, 21.
21. "Forefather's Song."
22. Freidel, *Changing Ideas About Women*, 141.
23. Ibid.
24. John Naisbitt, *Megatrends* (New York: Warner Books, 1984), 261.

Chapter 4—From Patriarch to Patriot

1. G. Gorer, *The American People: A Study of National Character* (New York: Norton, 1948).
2. Charles Sumner, *Prophetic Voices Concerning America* (Boston: Lee & Shepard, 1974), 112–13.
3. Ibid., 113.
4. Stearns, *Be A Man*, 51.
5. Elizabeth A. Moize, "Daniel Boone: First Hero of the Frontier," *National Geographic*, December 1985, 819.
6. Stearns, *Be A Man*, 51.
7. Freidel, *Changing Ideas*, 68.
8. Lawrence H. Fuchs, *Family Matters* (New York: Random House, 1972), 19.
9. Douglas, *Feminization*, 50.
10. Ryan, *Womanhood*, 84, 85.
11. Stearns, *Be A Man*, 48.
12. Ryan, *Womanhood*, 73.
13. Stearns, *Be A Man*, 44.
14. Ibid., 53.
15. Ibid., 63.
16. Sumner, *Prophetic Voices*, 61.
17. Douglas, *Feminization*, 24.
18. Ibid.
19. Terry Somerville, "Hero or Heretic," *Again*, vol. 6, no. 1, 17.
20. Stearns, *Be A Man*, 50.
21. Ibid.
22. Jane Rendall, *The Origins of Modern Feminism* (Houndsmill, England: Macmillan, 1985), 77.
23. Freidel, *Changing Ideas*, 151.
24. Douglas, *Feminization*, 52.
25. Freidel, *Changing Ideas*, 146.
26. Ibid.
27. Barbara Leslie Epstein, *The Politics of Domesticity* (Middletown, Conn.: Wesleyan University Press, 1981), 45.
28. Ibid., 51.
29. Rendall, *Modern Feminism*, 78.

30. Ibid.
31. Ibid.
32. Bernard A. Weisberger, *They Gathered at the River* (Boston: Little, Brown, & Co., 1958), 94, 96.
33. Kari Torjesen Malcolm, *Women at the Crossroads* (Downers Grove, Ill.: Inter-Varsity, 1982), 122.
34. Epstein, *Politics of Domesticity*, 59.
35. Ibid., 61.
36. Ibid.
37. Ibid.
38. Rendall, *Modern Feminism*, 82.
39. Ibid., 78.
40. Malcolm, *Women at the Crossroads*, 122.

Chapter 5—Victoria's Secrets

1. Ruth Bordin, *Women and Temperance* (Philadelphia: Temple University Press, 1981), 18.
2. Herbert Ashby, *Carry Nation* (New York: Knopf, 1929), 108.
3. Ibid., 121.
4. Ryan, *Womanhood*, 115.
5. Ibid., 114–15.
6. Freidel, *Changing Ideas*, 170.
7. Brenton, *American Male*, 136.
8. Freidel, *Changing Ideas*, 168.
9. Rendall, *Modern Feminism*, 74–75.
10. Ryan, *Womanhood*, 114.
11. Douglas, *Feminization*, 82.
12. Stearns, *Be A Man*, 87.
13. Ibid., 86.
14. Ibid.
15. Fuchs, *Family Matters*, 109.
16. Stearns, *Be A Man*, 107.
17. Ryan, *Womanhood*, 149.
18. Mary Earhart, *Frances Willard* (Chicago: University of Chicago Press, 1944), 98.
19. Patricia Sexton, *The Feminized Male* (New York: Random House, 1969), 29.
20. Hans Sebald, *Momism* (Chicago: Nelson-Hall, 1976), 111–12.
21. Nancy F. Cott, *The Bounds of Womanhood* (New Haven: Yale University Press, 1977), 132.
22. Ibid., 148.
23. Stearns, *Be A Man*, 87.
24. "Religion in America," *The Gallup Report* no. 222, March 1984, 76.
25. Cott, *Bounds of Womanhood*, 129–30.
26. Douglas, *Feminization*, 111–12.
27. Rufus B. Spain, *At Ease in Zion* (Nashville: Vanderbilt University Press, 1967), 169.
28. Cott, *Bounds of Womanhood*, 86.
29. Ibid., 85.

30. Ryan, *Womanhood*, 150.
31. Ibid., 151.
32. Ibid., 130.

Chapter 6—A Vanishing Breed

1. Partnow, *Quotable Woman*, 2:387.
2. Cole, *Maximized Manhood*, 142.
3. U.S. Bureau of the Census, *Statistical Abstract of the United States* (Washington, D.C.: Government Printing Office, 1985), 46.
4. U.S. Bureau of the Census, *Statistical Abstract of the United States* (Washington, D.C.: Government Printing Office, 1986), 56, 62.
5. Ibid., 59, 79, 80 .
6. Norman M. Lobsenz, "How to Make a Second Marriage Work," *Parade Magazine*, September 1, 1985, 12.
7. Alvin P. Sanoff, "Our Neglected Kids," *U.S. News and World Report*, August 9, 1982, 57.
8. David Elkind, "Youngsters Under Stress—What Parents Do," *U.S. News and World Report*, August 9, 1982, 58.
9. Cole, *Maximized Manhood*, 142.
10. Pierre Mornell, *Passive Men and Wild, Wild Women* (New York: Simon & Schuster, 1979).
11. Daniel Amneus, *Back to Patriarchy* (New Rochelle, N.Y.: Arlington House, 1979), 64.
12. Ibid.
13. Sebald, *Momism*, 58, 59.
14. John Leo, "Single Parent, Double Trouble," *Time*, January 4, 1982, 81.
15. Amneus, *Back to Patriarchy*, 64.
16. Abigail Wood, "The Trouble With Dad," *Seventeen*, October 1985, 38.
17. Dotson Rader, "Who Will Help The Children?" *Parade Magazine*, September 5, 1982, 5.

Chapter 7—Confessions of a Fish out of Water

1. Sexton, *Feminized Male*, 14.
2. Ibid., 10.
3. Sebald, *Momism*, 111–12.
4. Marlene Lefever, "Is Sunday School Losing Its Punch?" *Christianity Today*, September 21, 1979, 21.
5. Ibid.
6. Sexton, *Feminized Male*, 29.
7. Heron Marquez Estrada, "Drop-Out Woes Are Real Here," *Santa Cruz Sentinel*, March 3, 1986, A-1.
8. Channel 5 Eyewitness News, KPIX, San Francisco, September 17, 1985.
9. Sexton, *Feminized Male*, 13.

Chapter 8—It's a Crime to Be Male

1. "The Phil Donahue Show," KBSW, Monterey/Salinas, February 17, 1986.
2. Stearns, *Be A Man*, 116, 124.

3. Partnow, *Quotable Woman*, 2:252, 34.
4. Ibid., 2:289.
5. Sexton, *Feminized Male*, 7.
6. Donald MacGillis and ABC News, *Crime in America* (Radnor, Penn.: Chilton Book Co., 1983), 143.
7. U.S. Bureau of the Census, *Satistical Abstract—1985*, 182.
8. MacGillis, *Crime in America*, 143.
9. Gittelson, *Dominus*, 35.
10. Richard Stengel, "When Brother Kills Brother," *Time*, September 16, 1985, 33.
11. U.S. Bureau of the Census, *Statistical Abstract—1985*, 182.
12. MacGillis, *Crime in America*, 143.
13. U.S. Bureau of the Census, *Statistical Abstract—1985*, 173.
14. Amneus, *Back to Patriarchy*, 26, 64.
15. MacGillis, *Crime in America*, 32.
16. U.S. Bureau of the Census, *Statistical Abstract—1985*, 173.
17. KTVU-Channel 2, "Powder Keg Prisons."
18. MacGillis, *Crime in America*, 32.
19. Rochelle Distelheim, "Where Are All The Men For Women Like Us?" *The Working Woman*, November 1983, 142.
20. Ibid.
21. U.S. Bureau of the Census, *Statistical Abstract—1985*, 46.
22. U.S. Department of Justice, Bureau of Justice Statistics, *Sourcebook of Criminal Justice Statistics, 1983* (Washington, D.C.: Government Printing Office, 1984), 574.
23. Stengel, "When Brother Kills Brother," 32.
24. Ibid.
25. MacGillis, *Crime in America*, 63.
26. Ibid., 40.
27. Amneus, *Back to Patriarchy*, 54.
28. MacGillis, *Crime in America*, 40.
29. Charles Murray, *Losing Ground: American Social Policy 1950–1980* (New York: Basic Books, 1984), 160.
30. William Johnston, *King* (New York: Warner Books, 1978), 200.

Chapter 9—A Model for Manhood

1. 2 Thessalonians 2:15.
2. Job 1:5.
3. Clayton C. Barbeau, *The Head of the Family* (Chicago: Henry Regnery Co., 1961), xiii.
4. Ephesians 4:26.
5. Richard Ballew, *Coming in from the Cold* (Mt. Hermon, Calif.: Conciliar Press, 1978), 2.
6. Job 1:8.
7. Job 1:21.

Chapter 10—Father Is Not a Four-Letter Word

1. J. Richard Ballew, personal conversation with the author on May 5, 25, 1985.

2. Malachi 4:5–6, italics added.
3. Psalm 68:5.
4. Isaiah 9:6.
5. John 14:9.
6. Subcommittee of the Ecumenical Task Force of the Orthodox Church in America, *Women and Men in the Church* (Syosset, N.Y.: Department of Religious Education, Orthodox Church in America, 1980), 49.
7. John 14:6.
8. Ephesians 3:14–15. "Fatherhood" is a better translation of the Greek that appears as "the whole family" in the NKJV.
9. Thomas Howard, *Splendor in the Ordinary* (Wheaton, Ill.: Tyndale, 1976), 53.
10. Exodus 4:22.
11. Isaiah 63:16; 64:8; Jeremiah 3:19; and elsewhere.
12. 1 Chronicles 28:6.
13. Psalm 68:5.
14. John 17:3.
15. 1 Corinthians 8:6.
16. "To Manipulate A Housewife" (San Diego: Concerned Women for America, 1979), 221.
17. Hebrews 13:17.
18. Ryan, *Womanhood*, 44.
19. John 14:9.

Chapter 11—Marks of Manly Love

1. Dan Kiley, *The Peter Pan Syndrome* (New York: Dodd, Mead, 1983), 22.
2. Mark 1:11.
3. John 17:26.
4. John 3:16.
5. 1 John 3:1.
6. 1 John 4:19, italics added.
7. Ephesians 5:25.
8. 1 Corinthians 13:7.
9. Ibid.
10. Ibid.
11. Colossians 3:14.
12. U.S. Bureau of the Census, *Statistical Abstract (1986)*, 182.
13. Naisbitt, *Megatrends*, 261.
14. Amatae Etzione.
15. Zechariah 8:2.
16. Isaiah 42:13.
17. Isaiah 37:32.
18. Isaiah 9:6–7.
19. Ballew, *Coming in from the Cold*, 10.
20. Luke 2:48, italics added.
21. Luke 2:49.
22. Luke 2:51–52.
23. Ephesians 6:1.

24. James Dobson, *Focus on the Family Film Series*, Film 3—"Christian Fathering" (Waco, Tex.: Word, 1979).
25. 1 Corinthians 4:15–16.

Chapter 12—Returning to Manhood

1. 1 Timothy 6:12.
2. John 4:23, italics added.
3. John 15:26.
4. Luke 24:49.
5. John 2:16.
6. Ephesians 5:25.
7. Jack Sparks, *The Apostolic Fathers* (Nashville: Thomas Nelson, 1978), 93.
8. Mark 10:8–9.
9. Malachi 2:16.
10. 1 Corinthians 4:16.
11. Hamilton, *Father's Influence*, 77–78.
12. C. William Blythe, "When Happiness Becomes an Idol," *Again*, vol. 7, no. 1, 15.
13. Joshua 24:15.

Selected Bibliography

Amneus, Daniel. *Back to Patriarchy*. New Rochelle, N.Y.: Arlington House, 1979.

Andelin, Aubrey. *Man of Steel and Velvet*. Toronto: Bantam Books, 1983.

Annals of America. The, Vol. 1, *Discovering a New World, 1493–1754*. Encyclopaedia Britannica Inc., 1968.

Asbury, Herbert. *The Great Illusion*. Garden City, N.Y.: Doubleday, 1950.

Ashby, Herbert. *Carry Nation*. New York: Knopf, 1929.

Ballew, Richard. *Coming in from the Cold*. Mt. Hermon, Calif.: Conciliar Press, 1978.

Barbeau, Clayton C. *The Head of the Family*. Chicago: Henry Regnery Co., 1961.

Barrer, Myra E. *Women's Organizations & Leaders Directory—1975–76 Edition*. Washington, D.C.: Today Publications & News Service, 1975.

Beard, Mary R. *America Through Women's Eyes*. New York: Macmillan, 1933.

Behnke, Donna. *Religious Issues in Nineteenth Century Feminism*. Troy, N.Y.: Whitstone, 1982.

Benson, Mary Sumner. *Women in 18th Century America*. Port Washington: Kennikat Press, 1966.

Berg, Barbara J., *The Remembered Gate: Origins of American Feminism*. New York: Oxford University Press, 1978.

Bilezikian, Gilbert. *Beyond Sex Roles*. Grand Rapids, Mich.: Baker, 1985.

Blair, Henry William. *The Temperance Movement*. Boston: William Smythe Co., 1888.

Blocker, Jack S., Jr. *Give to the Winds thy Fears*. n.p., Conn.: Greenwood Press, 1985.

Bordin, Ruth. *Women and Temperance*. Philadelphia: Temple University Press, 1981.
Brenton, Myron. *The American Male*. New York: Coward-McCann, 1966.
Bustanoby, Andre. *Just Talk to Me*. Grand Rapids, Mich.: Zondervan, 1981.
Campolo, Tony. *You Can Make a Difference*. Waco, Tex.: Word, 1984.
Clark, Norman H. *Deliver Us From Evil*. New York: W. W. Norton & Co., 1976.
Clark, Stephen B. *Man and Woman in Christ*. Ann Arbor, Mich.: Servant Books, 1980.
Clarke, James W. *American Assassins*. Princeton, N.J.: Princeton University Press, 1982.
Cole, Edwin Louis. *Maximized Manhood*. Springdale, Penn.: Whitaker House, 1984.
Conley, Paul, and Andrew Sorenson. *The Staggering Steeple*. Philadelphia: Pilgrim Press, 1971.
Cott, Nancy F. *Root of Bitterness*. New York: Dutton, 1972.
———. *The Bonds of Womanhood*. New Haven: Yale University Press, 1977.
Coward, Rosalind. *Patriarchal Precedents*. London: Routledge & Kegan Paul, 1983.
Craven, Wesley Frank. *A History of the South*. Vol. 1, *The Southern Colonies in the 17th Century, 1607–1689*. Baton Rouge: Louisiana State University Press, 1949.
Cyclopaedia of Temperance and Prohibition. New York: Funk & Wagnalls, 1891.
Davis, Harold E. *The Fledgling Province*. Chapel Hill, N.C.: University of North Carolina Press, 1966.
Delamont, Sara, and Lorna Duffin. *The 19th Century Woman*. New York: Barnes & Noble, 1978.
Dexter, Elisabeth Anthony. *Colonial Women of Affairs, Before 1776*. Clifton, n.p.: Augustus M. Kelly, 1972.
Dingwall, Eric John. *The American Woman*. New York: Rinehart & Co., 1957.
Dobson, James. *What Wives Wish Their Husbands Knew About Women*. Wheaton, Ill.: Tyndale, 1975.
Douglas, Ann. *The Feminization of American Culture*. New York: Knopf, 1977.
Earhart, Mary. *Frances Willard*. Chicago: University of Chicago Press, 1944.
Earle, Alice Morse. *Home Life in Colonial Days*. New York: Grosset & Dunlap, 1898.
Elliot, Elisabeth. *The Mark of the Man*. Old Tappan, N.J.: Revell, 1981.
Epstein, Barbara Leslie. *The Politics of Domesticity*. Middletown, Conn.: Wesleyan University Press, 1981.
Evans, Colleen, and Louis Evans, Jr. *Bold Commitment*. Wheaton, Ill.: Victor Books, 1983.
Fiorenza, Elisabeth Schussler. *In Memory of Her*. New York: Crossroad, 1984.
Franklin, Clyde W., II. *The Changing Definition of Masculinity*. New York: Plenum Press, 1984.

Freidel, Frank. *Changing Ideas About Women in the United States, 1776–1825*. New York: Garland, 1981.

Fuchs, Lawrence H. *Family Matters*. New York: Random House, 1972.

Getz, Gene A. *The Measure of a Marriage*. Ventura, Calif.: Regal Books, 1984.

Gittelson, Natalie. *Dominus*. New York: Farrar, Straus & Giroux, 1978.

Goldberg, Steven. *The Inevitability of Patriarchy*. New York: William Morrow, 1974.

Graw, J. B. *The Life of Mrs. Downs*. Camden, N.J.: Gazette Printing and Publishing House, 1892.

Gundry, Patricia. *Heirs Together*. Grand Rapids, Mich.: Zondervan, 1980.

Hamilton, Marshall L. *Father's Influence on Children*. Chicago: Nelson-Hall, 1979.

Hammond, John L. *The Politics of Benevolence*. Norwood, N.J.: Ablex, 1979.

Horn, Maurice. *The World Encyclopedia of Comics*. New York: Chelsea House, 1976.

Houghton, Walter E. *The Victorian Frame of Mind*. New Haven: Yale University Press, 1978.

Howard, Thomas. *Splendor in the Ordinary*. Wheaton, Ill.: Tyndale, 1976.

Howe, Daniel Walker. *Victorian America*. Philadelphia: University of Pennsylvania Press, 1976.

Introducing the University. Berkeley: Office of the Assistant V.P.—Student Academic Services, UCB, 1985–86.

Johnston, William. *King*. New York: Warner Books, 1978.

Kiley, Dan. *The Peter Pan Syndrome*. New York: Dodd, Mead, 1983.

———. *The Wendy Dilemma*. New York: Arbor House, 1984.

Komarovsky, Mirra. *Dilemmas of Masculinity*. New York: W. W. Norton & Co. 1976.

Krout, John Allen. *The Origins of Prohibition*. New York: Russell & Russell, 1967.

Lasch, Christopher. *The Culture Narcissism*. New York: Warner Books, 1979.

Levitan, Sar A., and Richard S. Belous. *What's Happening to the American Family*. Baltimore: Johns Hopkins University Press, 1981.

Lichtenstein, Grace. *Machisma*. New York: Doubleday, 1981.

Longmate, Norman. *The Water-Drinkers*. London: Hamish Hamilton, 1968.

Lynn, Robert W., and Elliot Wright. *The Big Little School*. New York: Harper & Row, 1971.

MacDonald, Gordon. *The Effective Father*. Wheaton, Ill.: Tyndale, 1985.

MacGillis, Donald, and ABC News. *Crime in America*. Radnor, Penn.: Chilton Book Co., 1983.

Maclay, George, and Humphry Knipe. *The Dominant Man*. New York: Delacorte Press, 1972.

Malcolm, Kari Torjesen. *Women at the Crossroads*. Downers Grove, Ill.: Inter-Varsity, 1982.

Mander, Jerry. *Four Arguments for the Elimination of Television*. New York: Quill, 1978.

Mellen, Joan. *Big Bad Wolves*. New York: Pantheon Books, 1977.

Mitscherlich, Alexander. *Society Without the Father*. New York: Harcourt, Brace & World, 1963.

Montagu, Ashley. *The Natural Superiority of Women*. New York: Macmillan, 1957.

Morgan, Edmund S. *Virginians at Home*. New York: Holt, Rinehart & Winston, 1952.

Mornell, Pierre. *Passive Men and Wild, Wild, Women*. New York: Simon & Schuster, 1979.

Murray, Charles. *Losing Ground: American Social Policy 1950–1980*. New York: Basic Books, 1984.

Naisbitt, John. *Megatrends*. New York: Warner Books, 1984.

New American Standard Bible. La Habra. Calif.: Lockman Foundation, 1971.

New King James Version of the Bible. Nashville: Thomas Nelson, 1982.

Nickles, Elizabeth. *The Coming Matriarchy*. New York: Seaview Books, 1981.

O'Connor, Diane, and Dick O'Connor. *How to Make Your Man More Sensitive*. New York: Dutton, 1975.

Ossoli, Margaret Fuller. *Woman in the Nineteenth Century*. Boston: John P. Jewett & Co., 1857.

Ostrovsky, Everett A. *Children Without Men*. New York: Collier Books, 1966.

Packard, Vance. *Nation of Strangers*. New York: McKay, 1972.

Partnow, Elaine, ed. *The Quotable Woman*. 2 vols. Los Angeles: Pinnacle Books, 1977.

Payne, Leanne. *Crisis in Masculinity*. Westchester, Ill.: Crossway Books, 1985.

Polson, Beth, and Miller Newton. *Not My Kid*. New York: Arbor House, 1984.

Porterfield, Amanda. *Feminine Spirituality in America*. Philadelphia: Temple University Press, 1980.

Postman, Neil. *The Disappearance of Childhood*. New York: Laurel Books, 1982.

Rendall, Jane. *The Origins of Modern Feminism*. Houndsmill, England: Macmillan, 1985.

Ruderman, Judith. *D. H. Lawrence and the Devouring Mother*. Durham, N.C.: Duke University Press, 1984.

Ruether, Rosemary, and Eleanor McLaughlin. *Women of Spirit*. New York: Simon & Schuster, 1979.

Ryan, Mary P. *Womanhood in America*. New York: Franklin Watts, 1983.

Scanzoni, John. *Love and Negotiate*. Waco, Tex.: Word, 1979.

Schlafly, Phyllis. *The Power of the Positive Women*. New Rochelle, N.Y.: Arlington House, 1977.

Sebald, Hans. *Momism*. Chicago: Nelson-Hall, 1976.

Sexton, Patricia. *The Feminized Male*. New York: Random House, 1969.

Shapiro, Stephen A. *Manhood*. New York: G. P. Putnam's Sons, 1984.

Sheehan, Marion Turner. *The Spiritual Woman*. New York: Harper & Bros., 1955.

Simels, Steven. *Gender Chameleons*. New York: Timbre Books/Arbor House, 1985.

Skjei, Eric, and Richard Rabkin. *The Male Ordeal*. New York: G. P. Putnam's Sons, 1981.

Smith, David W. *The Friendless American Male*. Ventura, Calif.: Regal Books, 1983.

Snyder, Charles R. *Alcohol and the Jews*. Glencoe, Ill.: Yale Center of Alcohol Studies, 1958.

Spain, Rufus B. *At Ease in Zion*. Nashville: Vanderbilt University Press, 1967.

Sparks, Jack. *The Apostolic Fathers*. Nashville: Thomas Nelson, 1978.

Spruill, Julia Cherry. *Women's Life and Work in the Southern Colonies*. New York: Russell & Russell, 1969.

Stanton, Elizabeth Cady. *The Original Feminist Attack on the Bible (The Woman's Bible)*. Reprint. New York: Arno Press, 1974.

Stassinopoulos, Arianna. *The Female Woman*. New York: Random House, 1973.

Stearns, Peter N. *Be A Man*. New York: Holmes & Meier, 1979.

Stetson, Charlotte Perkins. *Women and Economics*. Boston: Small, Maynard, & Co., 1900.

Sumner, Charles. *Prophetic Voices Concerning America*. Boston: Lee & Shepard, 1974.

Sundelson, David. *Shakespeare's Restorations of the Father*. New Brunswick, N.J.: Rutgers University Press, 1983.

Taylor, Barbara. *Eve and the New Jerusalem*. London: Virago Press, 1983.

Taylor, Robert Lewis. *Vessel of Wrath*. New York: New American Library, 1966.

Toffler, Alvin. *The Third Wave*. Toronto: Bantam Books, 1982.

Trobisch, Walter. *The Misunderstood Man*. Downers Grove, Ill.: InterVarsity, 1983.

U.S. Bureau of the Census. *Statistical Abstract of the United States*. Washington, D.C.: Government Printing Office, 1985.

———. *Statistical Abstract of the United States*. Washington, D.C.: Government Printing Office, 1986.

U.S. Department of Justice, Bureau of Justice Statistics. *Sourcebook of Criminal Justice Statistics, 1983*. Washington, D.C.: Government Printing Office, 1984.

University of California Santa Cruz General Catalog. Santa Cruz, Calif.: UCSC Publication, 1984.

Weisberger, Bernard A. *They Gathered at the River*. Boston: Little, Brown, & Co., 1958.

White, David Manning, and Robert H. Abel. *The Funnies*. London: Collier-Macmillan, 1963.

Whitener, Daniel Jay. *Prohibition in North Carolina, 1715–1945*. Chapel Hill, N.C.: University of North Carolina Press, 1945.

Yankelovich, Daniel. *New Rules*. Toronto: Bantam Books, 1981.

Articles

Ansen, David. "An American Icon." *Newsweek*, July 22, 1985.

Beckett, Kathleen. "The Menswear Phenomenon." *Vogue*, August 1984, 156, 164.

Blythe, C. William. "When Happiness Becomes An Idol." *Again*.

Cohen, Susan. "The Gender Trap." *West: San Jose Mercury News*, August 25, 1985, 16–21.

Dilibeto, Giora. "Invasion of the Gender Blenders." *People*, April 23, 1984, 97.

Distelheim, Rochelle. "Where Are All The Men For Women Like Us?" *The Working Woman*, November 1983.

Elkind, David. "Youngsters Under Stress—What Parents Do." *U.S. News and World Report*, August 9, 1982.

"Elisabeth Elliot on . . . Submitting Your Love Life to God." *Again*, vol. 8, no. 2, 21–24.

Estrada, Heron Marquez. "Drop-Out Woes Are Real Here." *Santa Cruz Sentinel*, March 3, 1986.

"Get Them Back in School." *San Francisco Examiner*, September 19, 1985, A–20.

Jennings, Nicholas. "Blurring the Boundaries of Gender." *Macleans*, July 23, 1984, 44.

Karras, Alex. "The Real Men on TV—and the Wimps." *TV Guide*, August 17–24, 1986, 4–8.

Landers, Ann. "Daddy Was A Wimp." *Santa Cruz Sentinel*, October 25, 1984, B–5.

Lefever, Marlene. "Is Sunday School Losing Its Punch?" *Christianity Today*, September 21, 1979, 16–21.

Leo, John. "Single Parent, Double Trouble." *Time*, January 4, 1982.

———. "The Eleventh Megatrend." *Time*, July 23, 1984, 104.

Lewis, Gregg. "The Return of Apathy." *Christianity Today*, October 18, 1985, 21–25.

Lobsenz, Norman M. "How to Make a Second Marriage Work." *Parade Magazine*, September 1, 1985.

Moize, Elizabeth A. "Daniel Boone: First Hero of the Frontier." *National Geographic*, December 1985.

Rader, Dotson, "Who Will Help The Children?" *Parade Magazine*, September 5, 1982.

"Religion in America." *The Gallup Report* no. 222, March 1984.

Safran, Claire. "Why Men Hurt the Women They Love." *Reader's Digest*, January, 1986.

Sanoff, Alvin P. "Our Neglected Kids." *U.S. News and World Report*, August 9, 1982.

Somerville, Terry. "Hero or Heretic." *Again*, vol. 6, no. 1.

———. "The ERA: Something Missing." *Again*, January–March 1980, 9.

Stein, Benjamin J. "The New War Between Men and Women." *The American Spectator*, November 1985.

Stengel, Richard. "When Brother Kills Brother." *Time*, September 16, 1985.

"To Manipulate A Housewife." San Diego: Concerned Women for America, 1979.

Wallace, Mike. "Carroll O'Connor answers the tough questions about 'Archie Bunker.'" *Good Housekeeping*, October 1974.

Wood, Abigail. "The Trouble With Dad." *Seventeen*, October 1985.

Zell, Ray. "Revision or Perversion: An Attempt to De-Sex the Scriptures." *Again*, vol. 7, no. 1.

Television ━━━━━━━━━━━━━━━━━━━━━━━━━━━━━━━━━━━━

"The Phil Donahue Show," KBSW, Monterey/Salinas, February 17, 1986.

Channel 5 Eyewitness News, KPIX, San Francisco, September 17, 1985.

Film ━━

Dobson, James. *Focus on the Family Film Series*. Film 3—"Christian Fathering." Waco, Tex.: Word, 1979.